SINGER SIMPLE

home décor handbook

essential machine-side tips and techniques

the editors of Singer Worldwide

credits

Heather Brine Lambert has illustrated a variety of instructional books and magazine articles. She also applies her artistic bent to interior and home design. She resides in Massachusetts with her husband Dave, daughters April and Kara, and an assortment of dogs and cats

Creative Publishing international

Copyright 2007
Creative Publishing international
18705 Lake Drive East
Chanhassen, Minnesota 55317
1-800-328-3895
www.creativepub.com

President/CEO: Ken Fund

Vice President/Sales & Marketing: Peter Ackroyd

Executive Managing Editor: Barbara Harold

Acquisition Editor: Deborah Cannarella

Associate Editor: Beth Baumgartel

Senior Editor: Linda Neubauer

Creative Director: Michele Lanci-Altomare

Art Director: Jon Simpson

Production Manager: Laura Hokkanen

Cover and Book Design: Mary Rohl

Page Layout: Tina R. Johnson

Illustration: Heather Lambert

SINGER sewing machines are available at authorized SINGER retailers.

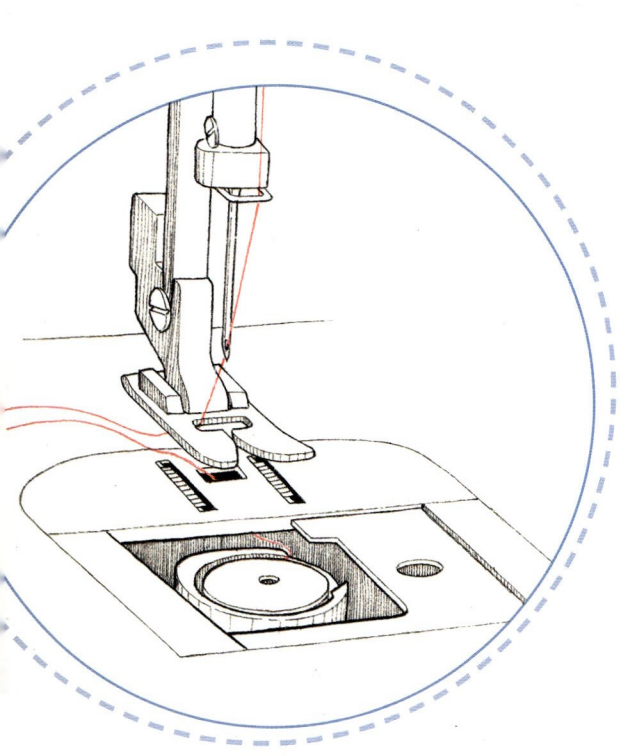

Library of Congress Cataloging-in-Publication Data

Singer Simple Home Décor Handbook :
essential machine-side tips and techniques.

    p. cm. -- (Singer simple)

  Singer At head of title:

Includes index.

  ISBN-13: 978-1-58923-314-0 (soft cover)
  ISBN-10: 1-58923-314-X (soft cover)

 1. House furnishings. 2. Sewing. I. Creative Publishing International. II.

Title: At head of title:. III. Series.

TT387.557 2007

  646.2'1--dc22   2006032901

Printed in China

10 9 8 7 6 5 4 3 2 1

Due to differing conditions, materials, and skill levels, the publisher and various manufacturers disclaim any liability for unsatisfactory results or injury due to improper use of tools, materials, or information in this publication.

contents

ready for a change?
Turn your decorating ideas into reality!

Wish you could give your home a makeover, but without all the disruption and expense? You don't need to hire a celebrity decorator. The best way to decorate—and the only way to get exactly what you want—is to do it yourself. And that's easier than you think!

With a few basic sewing tools, some fabulous fabrics, and a little imagination, you can give your home a fresh, new look. *Singer Simple Home Décor Handbook* will guide you through your creative choices and provide you with all the basics as you plan and sew.

Create curtains, throw pillows,

bed linens and shower curtains—with the fabrics and trims you love. Coordinate or contrast colors. Add a personal, decorative touch. Transform even the most basic shapes and projects with decorative patterns, textures, and trims. By sewing for your home, you can turn your vision into reality— and save money, too!

Singer Simple Home Décor Handbook is a quick and easy reference you'll want to keep handy as you plan and sew. It includes a brief overview of the sewing machine and serger and shows you all the basic tools and techniques for home décor sewing. Charts and checklists take the guesswork out of style and fabric selection. The sections are color-coded for easy reference, and the text is illustrated with clear and informative illustrations. *Singer Simple Home Décor Handbook* will help you choose the projects, fabrics, and details to transform every room in your house and bring out the creative designer in you!

the sewing machine

All sewing machines are not created equal, although they all do basically the same thing. They interlock the top thread and the bobbin thread quickly and precisely to form stitches.

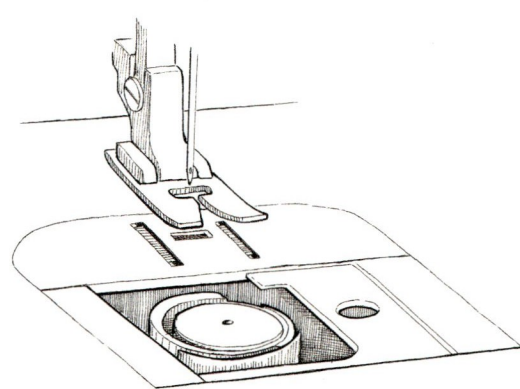

The top thread is threaded through the machine through a series of guides that control the thread's tension. The bottom thread is wound onto a bobbin.

Bobbins are small metal or plastic spools that fit under the throat plate. Some machines have a front- or side-loading bobbin, which also has a bobbin case. Other machines have top-loading (or top-drop-in) bobbins, which are inserted directly into the machine.

Computerized machines have a lot of automated features and a huge selection of utility and decorative stitches. All the bells and whistles are nice, but when you sew for your home, all you really need are a straight and a zigzag stitch.

Study your owner's manual to learn about all of your machine's features, so you can maximize its efficiency and your creative potential.

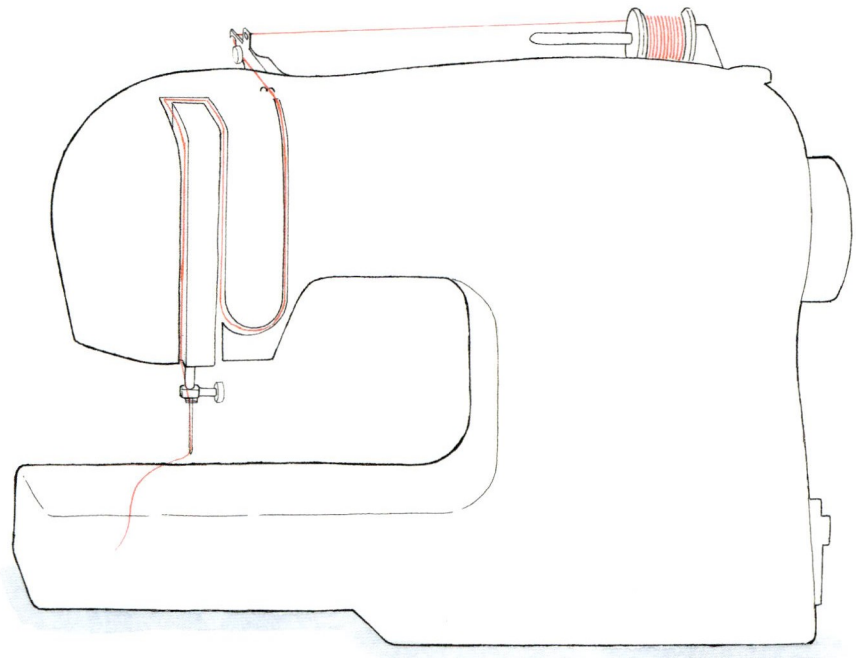

machine
features

Every model of machine has its own unique style and capabilities. Home décor sewing is a breeze when your sewing machine has special features like these.

automatic needle threader	button or lever that inserts the thread through the eye of the needle
automatic presser foot pressure	automatically adjusts for different fabric thicknesses
automatic thread cutter	cuts top and bottom threads when a button or knob is pushed or turned
buttonhole control knob	programs the machine to make buttonholes (some machines feature automatic, one-step buttonholes)
free arm	a small sewing area for tubular items, requires machine bed adjustment
LED or LCD screen	provides information and guidance but does not adjust or control the machine
LCD touch screen	allows you to adjust computerized-machine settings by touch
low bobbin indicator	beeps or flashes when the bobbin thread is low
needle stop up/down	presets the needle to stop in the up or down position, as needed
presser foot	keeps the fabric flat and guides it over the feed dogs.
presser foot knee-lift lever	allows you to lift the presser foot with your knee so you can keep your hands on your work
stitch length and width regulator	adjusts stitch size from 0 to 7 mm wide and from 0 to 6 mm long (range varies by machine)
thread guides	series of guides that control the upper thread to help form stitches and balance tension
throat plate	fits over the feed dogs and usually marked with seam allowance lines
variable stitch speed	allows you to speed up the machine for long, repetitive sewing or slow it down for precise, intricate work

machine needles

Always use the sewing machine needles recommended by the manufacturer of your sewing machine (or serger). This information is in your machine's manual. Keep an assortment of needle sizes in your supply box.

The upper portion of the sewing machine needle is called the shank, and the lower portion is called the shaft. Usually, the flat side of the needle shank faces the back of the machine (check your manual). If you insert the needle incorrectly, your stitches will be inconsistent and you could damage the machine.

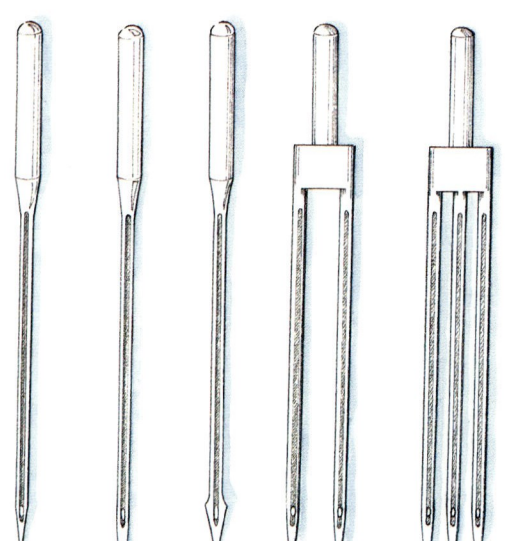

Needle Style

There are several needle styles for construction and decorative sewing. The type and weight of the fabric determines which size and style needle you should use.

sharp point needles: for woven fabrics—the sharp point pierces the fabric cleanly

ballpoint needles: for knit fabrics—the rounded tip slips through the knit fabric loops

wedge point needles: for leather—the wedge cuts a tiny slit for each stitch

twin or triple needles: for two or three parallel rows of stitches

Needle Size

Needle size is indicated by two numbers—the American sizes (9, 11, 12, 14, 16, 18) and the European sizes (60, 70, 80, 90, 100, 110)—with the smaller numbers representing thinner needles. As a general rule, the heavier the fabric, the larger the needle you'll need to sew. The most widely used needle sizes are 12/80 and 14/90.

If you aren't sure which size to use, start with 12/80. If the needle breaks or the thread shreds, try a larger size. If the seam puckers or the machine skips stitches, you may need a smaller needle.

Start every sewing project with a new needle, or change the needle after eight hours of sewing. Dull needles cause skipped stitches and snagged fabric.

presser feet

The right presser foot helps you sew faster, with a more consistent stitch. Every machine is sold with at least a few different feet. You can buy additional feet for special purposes, just make sure they attach the same way and have the right shank style for your machine.

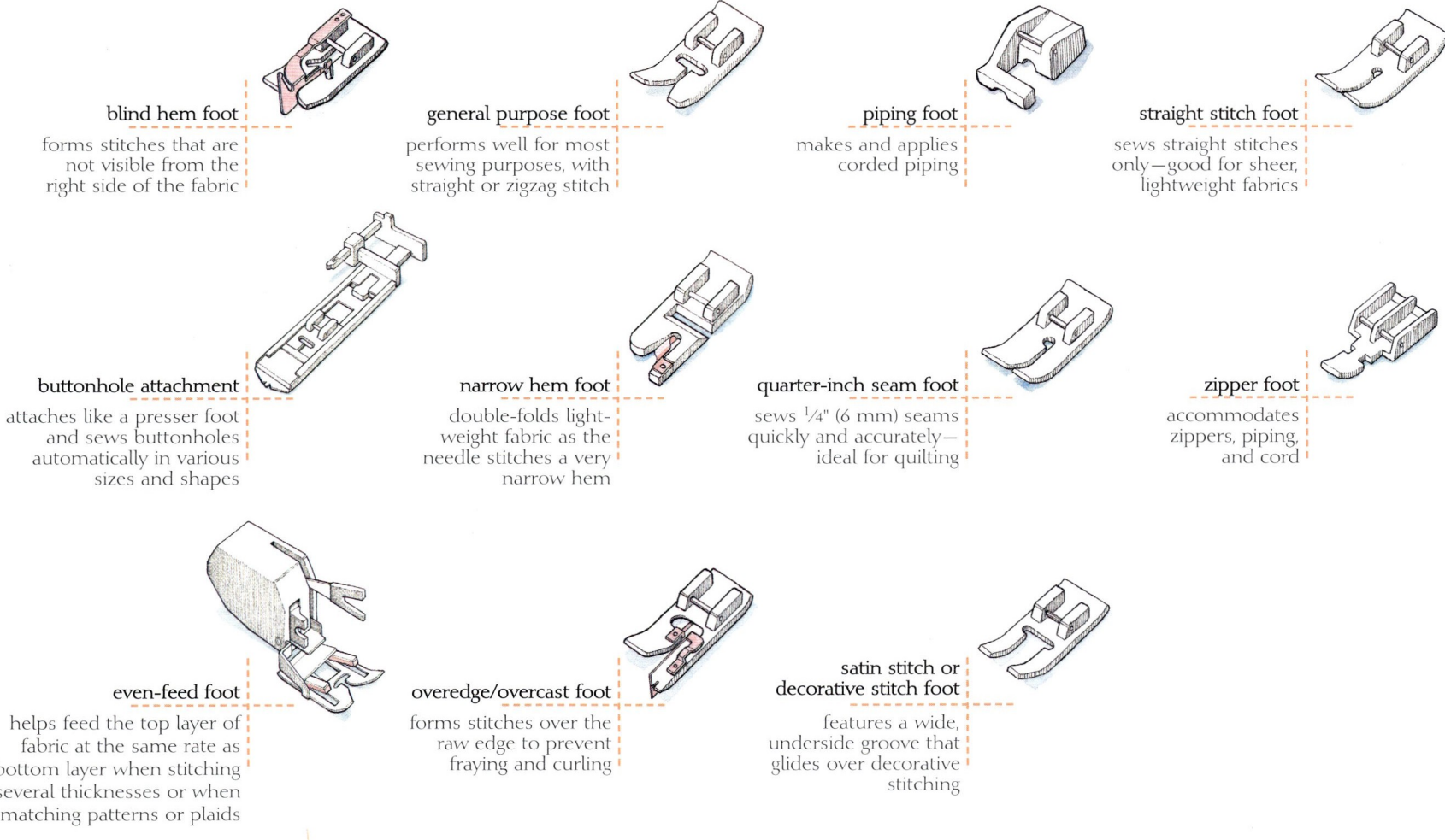

blind hem foot

forms stitches that are not visible from the right side of the fabric

general purpose foot

performs well for most sewing purposes, with straight or zigzag stitch

piping foot

makes and applies corded piping

straight stitch foot

sews straight stitches only—good for sheer, lightweight fabrics

buttonhole attachment

attaches like a presser foot and sews buttonholes automatically in various sizes and shapes

narrow hem foot

double-folds light-weight fabric as the needle stitches a very narrow hem

quarter-inch seam foot

sews $\frac{1}{4}$" (6 mm) seams quickly and accurately—ideal for quilting

zipper foot

accommodates zippers, piping, and cord

even-feed foot

helps feed the top layer of fabric at the same rate as bottom layer when stitching several thicknesses or when matching patterns or plaids

overedge/overcast foot

forms stitches over the raw edge to prevent fraying and curling

satin stitch or decorative stitch foot

features a wide, underside groove that glides over decorative stitching

specialty accessories

There are several specialty attachments that make home décor sewing easier. Here are a few you might like to try.

bias binder:

- folds and attaches bias binding to unfinished edge in one step
- works with premade bias or self-fabric bias-cut strips

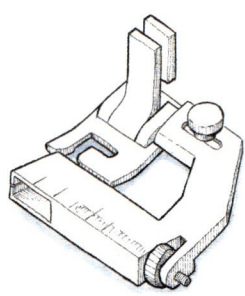

ruffler:

- folds fabric to form evenly spaced gathers or pleats
- some styles gather/pleat and attach to fabric in one step
- best for light- to medium-weight fabrics

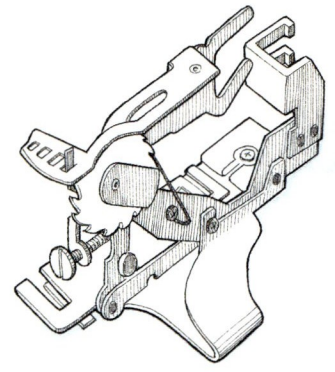

seam guide:

- attaches to machine bed with screw or magnet
- guides edge of fabric so seam allowance is consistent
- provides wider seam guide than the standard marks on the throat plate

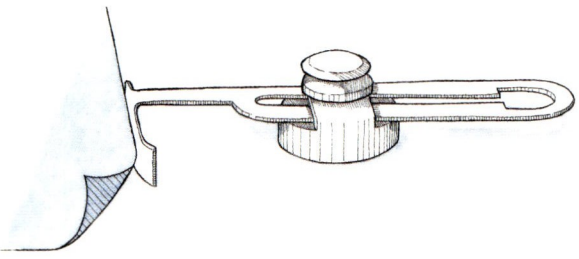

quilting guide bar:

- attaches directly to a quilting foot (and usually sold together)
- guides parallel rows of stitching, for channel quilting and topstitching

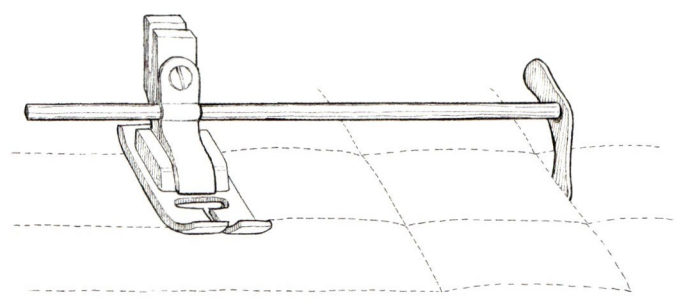

the serger

The serger—also called an overlock machine—creates a professional-looking edge finish on home fashions. It sews, trims, and overcasts the fabric edge in one step at a very high speed (about 1,600 stitches per minute).

Of course, you still need your sewing machine, but the serger is helpful for some types of construction and embellishment and for finishing seam allowances. Most have a differential feed feature that prevents puckers and stretched seams.

The major difference among sergers is the number of threads they can handle. They have either one or two needles and two or three loopers. Loopers work together with the needles to form the stitches in much the same way the bobbin works with the needle on the sewing machine. You can thread the loopers with decorative threads for special effects. Always thread the serger needles with utility thread.

All sergers sew a basic, three-thread overlock stitch, which is ideal for edge-finishing and for seaming knit fabrics.

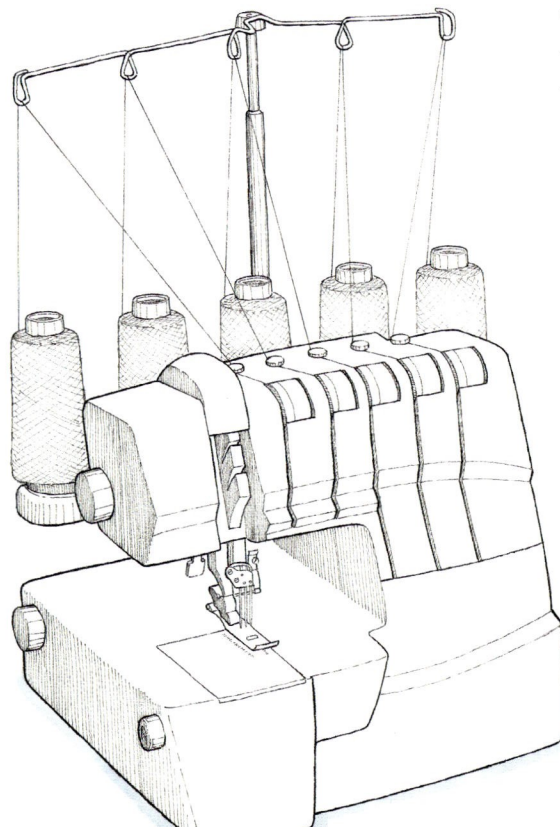

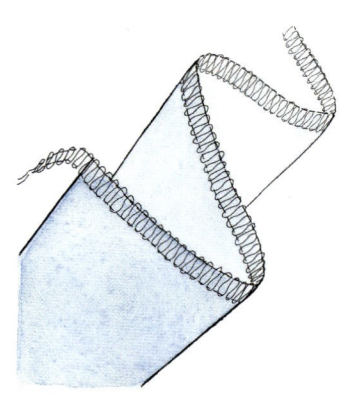

To secure the thread ends of a serged seam:
- dab on liquid fray preventer or fabric glue
- lift the presser foot, flip the fabric, and stitch over the last few stitches
- weave a long thread tail through the stitches with a tapestry needle

serger stitches

To form stitches, sergers use two, three, four, or five threads, which run through one or two needles and two or three loopers. The loopers deliver the thread to interlock with the needle threads—but they do not pierce the fabric. Instead, the looper threads sit on the top or underside of the fabric and wrap around the fabric's cut edge.

With your serger, you can sew and clean-finish window treatments, bed and bath linens, tablecloths, and pillows. Overlock and overedge stitches add strength, stability, and a more professional-looking finish. Other stitches, such as the flatlock and cover stitch, are more suitable for garment construction and embellishment.

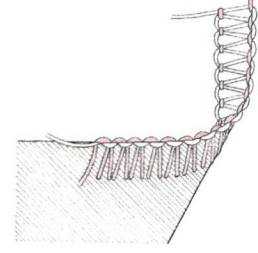

two-thread overedge

for lightweight seam finishing only, woven fabrics

threading: one needle, one looper

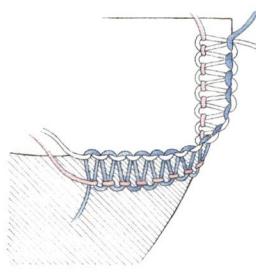
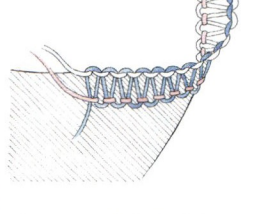

three-thread overlock

most common stitch, for seaming knit fabrics only, edge-finishing woven fabrics

threading: one needle, two loopers

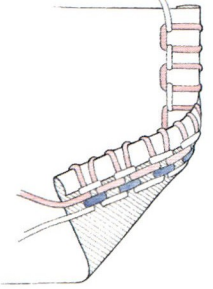

rolled edge

for hemming lightweight fabrics with fine edgestitching

threading: one needle, one or two loopers

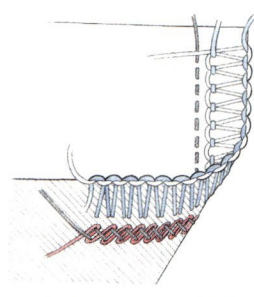

five-thread safety

for seaming and overcast-stitching woven fabrics

threading: two needles, three loopers

four-thread safety

for seaming and overedge-stitching; ideal for lightweight woven fabrics

threading: two needles, two loopers

all about thread

High-quality thread might be your most important sewing tool! It should be smooth and strong with uniform thickness. Color is the most obvious difference between threads, but the fiber content is equally important. As a general rule, match the fiber content of the thread with that of the fabric. Use the same type of thread in the needle and in the bobbin (unless you are sewing with decorative thread).

Common Threads

Cotton-wrapped polyester thread	Cotton thread	Polyester thread	Silk thread
• general-purpose thread • used for most sewing and dressmaking • suitable for natural or man-made fibers, knit, or woven fabrics	• best with cotton, linen, or wool fibers • good with woven fabrics	• suitable for fabrics made of man-made fibers, especially knits	• expensive • suitable for sewing on silk and wool fabric

Specialty Threads

Basting thread	Hand-quilting thread	Invisible thread	Machine embroidery thread	Metallic thread	Serger thread	Topstitching thread	Upholstery thread
• lightweight thread, usually 100 percent cotton • used for temporary stitches • breaks easily so you can pull out the stitches	• has a waxy coating to prevent tangles • strong enough to pass through multiple layers of fabric	• usually nylon • used for mending, machine-quilting, and attaching trim	• high-gloss thread • available in a crayon-box assortment of colors, textures, and sizes • designed to fill a specific area smoothly	• has a lovely shimmer • ideal for decorative stitching	• sold on large cones • designed for high-speed sewing • decorative threads, such as wooly nylon, nylon, metallic, cotton, and rayon, can be threaded in loopers	• strong and heavy • produces a well-defined stitch • works well for sewing on buttons	• 100 percent nylon or polyester • strong and resistant to chemicals and mildew • suitable for upholstery fabrics

interfacing & fusible web

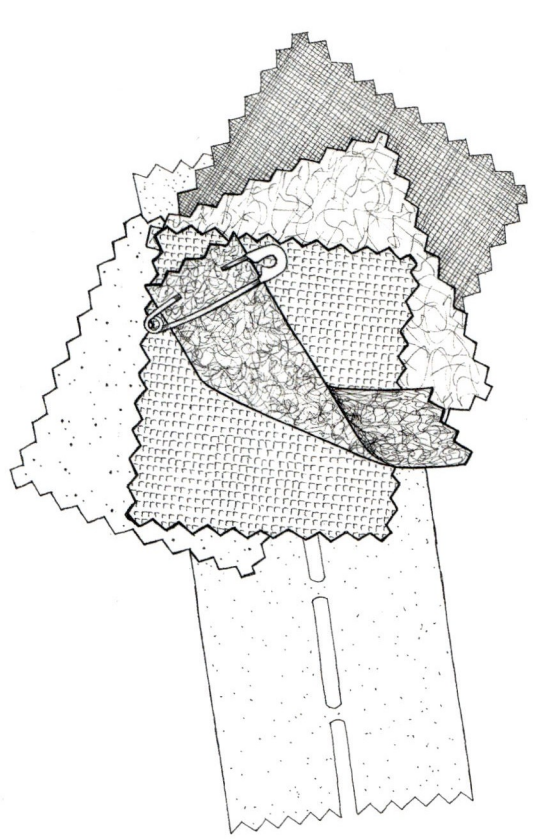

Interfacing is sewn or fused to the wrong side of a fabric to give the fabric extra body, stability, and stiffness. Decorator fabrics are usually strong and stable, but a lightweight fabric may need some additional support.

Interfacing can also be used to strengthen a specific area—such as a hem, top heading, or curtain tiebacks. It's best to apply an interfacing whose weight is compatible with the weight of the fabric.

Interfacings are either woven or nonwoven constructions, requiring either sew-in or fusible application. Woven sew-in interfacing tends to look more natural. It's also the best choice for fabric that can't withstand high heat.

Fusible, iron-on interfacing has a resin on one side, which bonds to the wrong side of the fabric. Fusible web is a sheet of adhesive that you place between two layers of fabric. It is available in narrow strips for hemming or in large pieces for fusing larger areas. It comes with or without paper backing.

Keep in mind that fusibles do change the hand—or feel—of the fabric. For light- and medium-weight interfacing, catch the interfacing in the seam. Heavy interfacing adds more bulk, so trim it to fit just inside the seam line.

Always test fusible interfacing or fusible web on a scrap piece of your project fabric.

sew-in, lightweight interfacing: Hand- or machine-baste the interfacing to the wrong side of the fabric, next to the seam line and inside the seam allowance. Trim away the interfacing close to the stitching.

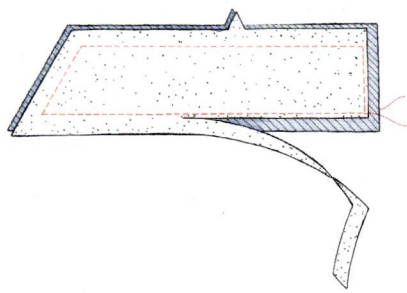

sew-in, medium- to heavy-weight interfacing: Trim the interfacing to fit inside the seam line and hand-baste it to the wrong side, to minimize bulk in the seam.

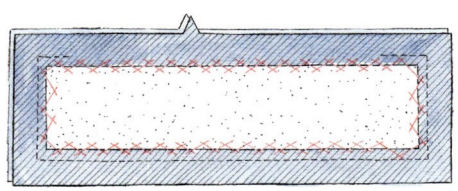

fusible interfacing: Place the interfacing adhesive side down on the wrong side of the fabric. Cover it with a damp press cloth. With a dry iron on a warm setting, press (do not iron) one area for about 15 seconds. Lift the iron, reposition it, and repeat the pressing until the whole piece is fused in place.

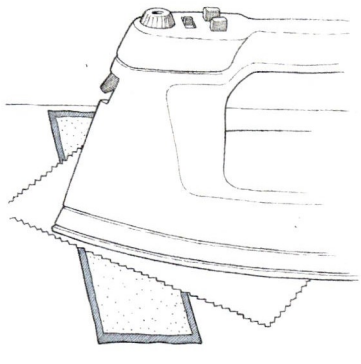

fusible web: Fusible web is placed between two fabrics to bond them together. Methods and heat settings differ from brand to brand, so follow the manufacturer's directions for application.

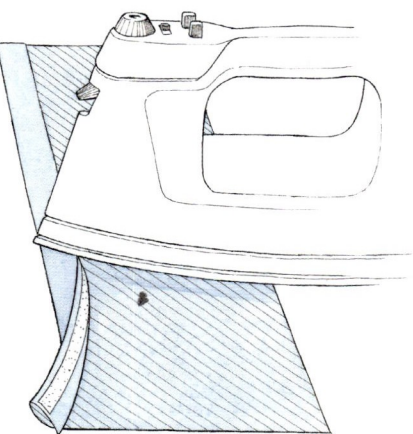

lining & interlining

Lining creates a professional, custom-made finish for your home décor. Drapery lining fabrics are available in the same widths as decorator fabrics. They are treated to resist stains and repel water, and some also block light.

For items like table runners or placemats, which have visible linings, choose lighter weight decorator fabric that has the same care requirements as the main fabric. (For instructions on how to line curtains, see pages 69-70; for placements, see page 51.)

What Does a Lining Do?

• protects the decorator fabric from soil and abrasion

• improves the way the item hangs or drapes

• neatens the wrong side and hides construction details

• adds to the longevity of the item

• protects decorator fabric from fading with sunlight

• helps maintain shape and provides stability

• gives windows a neat appearance from the outside

• blackout linings block light and increase opacity

• thermal lining adds insulation

Interlining is a fabric that is inserted and stitched between the main fabric and the lining. It adds extra body and insulation. It also makes fabrics with a printed design more opaque when light shines through. Plain drapery lining fabric can serve as interlining.

trims

Trims are the creative extras that give your projects a designer's touch and a custom finish. When selecting trims, make sure they have the same care requirements as the decorator fabric. It is easiest to categorize trims by the way they are applied to the fabric.

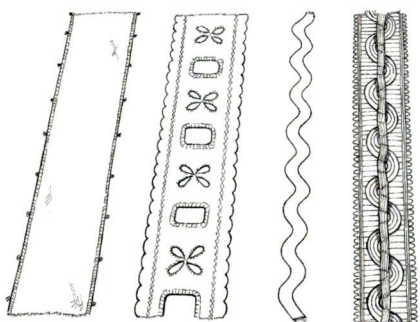

applied trims: band trim, beading, braid, gimp, ribbon, or any trim that is finished on both sides and sewn by hand or machine to the right side of the fabric

bias binding & fold-over braid: decorative and functional trims that encase raw edges; can be purchased ready-made or made from bias strips of fabric (page 96)

edgings: flat or gathered trim with one decorative edge (the unfinished edge is caught in a seam or hem); includes eyelet, fringe, lace, and ruffles

welting: fabric-covered cording or decorative cord attached to a braided tape; adds decorative accent to outer edges of a project and strengthens the seams

tassels: decorative elements in assorted styles and sizes

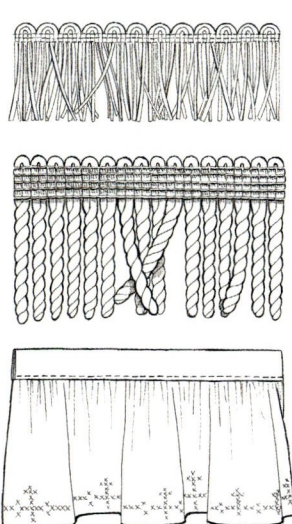

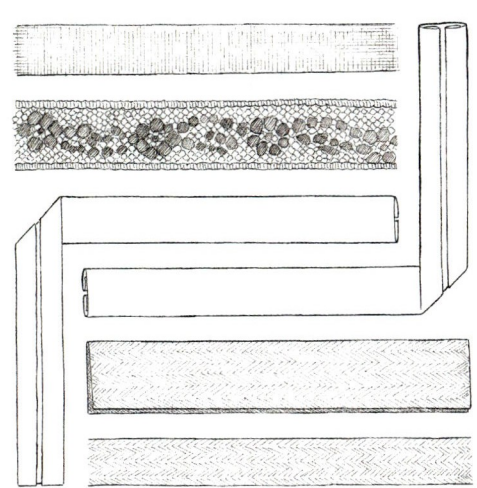

choosing the right fabric

Here's an at-a-glance guide that will help you choose fabrics for your home decorating projects. For specific care instructions, always check the labels on the fabric tubes—fiber content may affect the care requirements.

Fabric	Weight	Formal/Informal	Common Uses	Durable	Care
Antique Satin	Heavy	Formal	Draperies, upholstery, cushions, tablecloth	Yes	Dry-clean
Batiste	Light	Formal/informal	Under curtains, casual curtains, balloon shades	No	Machine wash
Broadcloth	Light to medium	Informal	Curtains, soft shades, bed linens, pillows, cushions, table linens, shower curtains	Yes	Machine wash
Brocade	Heavy	Formal	Draperies, bedcovers, pillows, cushions, tablecloth	Yes	Dry-clean
Calico	Light to medium	Informal	Curtains, pillows, table linens	Yes	Machine wash
Chintz	Medium to heavy	Formal/informal	Curtains, draperies, upholstery, shower curtains, cushions, Roman shades	Yes	Dry-clean
Damask	Medium	Formal	Draperies, upholstery, bedcovers, tablecloths	Yes	Machine wash or dry-clean
Dimity	Light	Formal	Under curtains, soft shades	No	Machine wash
Duck	Heavy	Informal	Draperies, slipcovers, Roman shades	Yes	Machine wash or dry-clean
Gingham	Light	Informal	Curtains, soft shades, tablecloths, napkins	Yes	Machine wash
Lawn	Light	Formal	Curtains, under curtains, pillows, napkins	Yes	Machine-wash
Lace	Light	Formal	Curtains, tablecloth	Varies	Machine wash or dry-clean

Fabric	Weight	Formal/Informal	Common Uses	Durable	Care
Matelasse	Heavy	Formal	Draperies, upholstery	Yes	Dry-clean
Moiré	Light to medium	Formal	Draperies, curtains, tablecloths	Yes	Machine-wash or dry-clean
Muslin	Light	Informal	Curtains, table linens, linings	No	Machine-wash
Organdy	Light	Formal/informal	Curtains, under curtains	No	Machine-wash
Percale	Medium	Informal	Curtains, bed linens, table linens	Yes	Machine-wash
Sateen	Light to medium	Formal	Curtains, bed linens, table linens, draperies	Yes	Machine-wash
Satin	Medium to heavy	Formal	Draperies, curtains, pillows, bed linens, Roman shades, upholstery	Yes	Machine-wash or dry-clean
Shantung	Light to medium	Formal	Draperies, curtains	Yes	Dry-clean
Suede cloth	Heavy	Formal/informal	Cushions, draperies, upholstery	Yes	Dry-clean
Taffeta	Light to medium	Formal	Draperies	Yes	Machine-wash or dry-clean
Velvet	Medium to heavy	Formal	Draperies, upholstery	No	Dry-clean
Voile	Light	Informal	Curtains, under curtains, balloon shades	No	Machine-wash

prepare your fabric

Preshrink your fabric—and lining, zipper, and trims—so the finished project won't shrink later. Launder everything as you intend to launder the finished item. Thoroughly steam-press any fabric that will be dry-cleaned. Machine-wash washable fabric in cold water with mild detergent and machine-dry.

Check the care instructions printed on the end of the fabric bolt. Machine-washing is convenient, but it may remove sizing and other finishes that enhance the fabric's beauty and performance.

If you aren't sure whether your fabric is washable, launder a 6" (15.2 cm) square. Remove it from the dryer, press, and measure. Is it still 6" (15.2 cm) square? Did it fade? Did it ravel? If the results are good, preshrink the entire length of fabric the same way.

If the fabric ravels, zigzag-stitch the cut edges before laundering. Press the dried fabric to eliminate wrinkles. Carefully press out the crease that formed on the bolt.

If the fabric can't be laundered, steam to preshrink it or have it dry-cleaned. To preshrink with steam, first steam-press a small scrap of the fabric to test for damage. Dampen the fabric (or a press cloth) and press on the wrong side until the water evaporates. Shoot steam into the fibers as you press.

If your fabric is identical on both sides, choose one side as the right side and then mark the wrong side with tailor's chalk or a fabric-marking pen so you won't confuse the sides when sewing.

Don't use the selvage as an edge. For projects that require full fabric widths, trim away the selvages before or after seaming or before hemming sides.

Determine whether the surface fibers have a definite up and down direction. Cut fabrics that have nap, pile, shine, shading, and one-way printed or woven designs so the fibers in all the pieces run the same direction (page 22).

Find the straight grain of the fabric and straighten the cut ends (page 21).

Dry-clean window treatments and machine-wash bed, bath, and table linens and pillow covers.

straightening fabric grain

Grain refers to the direction of the fabric threads. Lengthwise grain is parallel to the selvage. Crosswise grain is perpendicular to the selvage. Bias grain is diagonal, and the grain of a fabric with "true bias" runs 45 degrees to the lengthwise and crosswise grains.

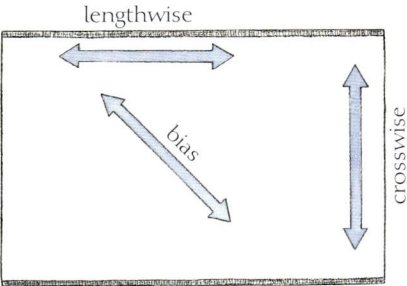

Woven fabric must be "on-grain"—with lengthwise and crosswise threads at right angles to each other. If not, curtains will hang crooked and seat cushions will look uneven. Here's how to check and straighten the grain:

1. Snip into the selvage and pull a crosswise thread so the fabric puckers. Cut along the puckered thread to the opposite selvage. The cut creates a perfectly straight grainline in the crosswise direction.

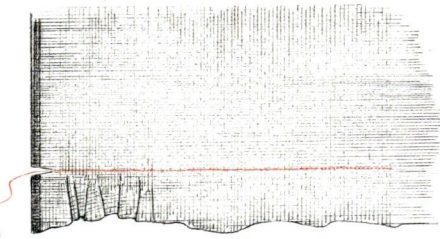

2. Fold the fabric in half lengthwise, aligning the selvages, and smooth it flat. Sometimes, you may need to gently pull the fabric corners to realign the ends. The cut ends should be even. If the ends don't align, shift the layers until they do. Pin the layers together along the selvages and ends at frequent intervals. Steam-press the fabric to align the fibers along the grainline.

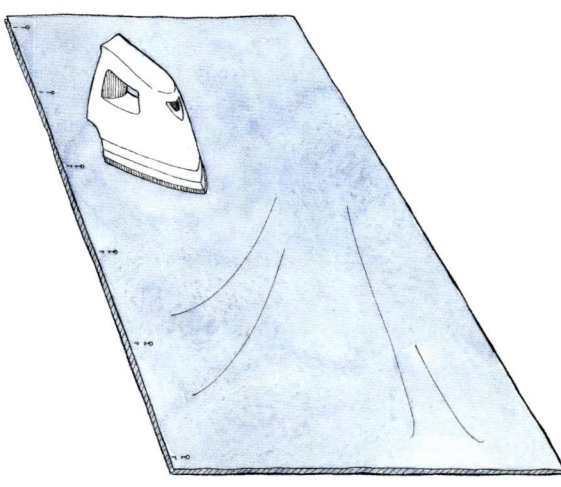

Once you are sure your fabric is on-grain, make all crosswise cuts perpendicular to the selvages, using a carpenter's square or T-square. Align one side of the ruler with the selvage and mark the perpendicular side with tailor's chalk. Cut along the marked line.

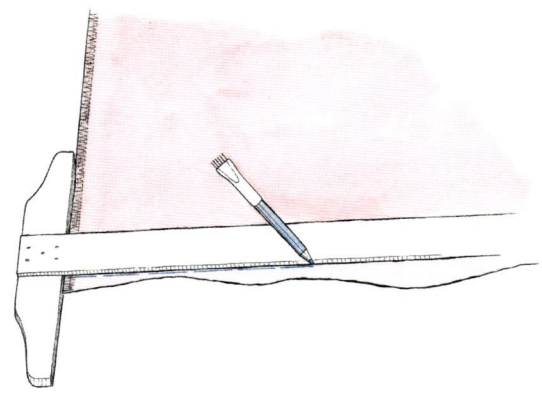

cutting the fabric

You can sew home décor items without paper patterns, especially large items like draperies and tablecloths—but, if you prefer, you can find patterns with step-by-step instructions for anything you want to make. In either case, the key to home décor sewing is careful measuring and cutting.

Prepare the Fabric for Cutting

Work on a large, flat surface so you can lay out the fabric straight and smooth. For most home décor projects, the fabric is cut in a single layer, with the right side up. This layout makes it easy to position and match design motifs.

If the fabric is directional, either because of surface nap or a one-way design (or if you're not sure), mark the top of the fabric and place all pattern pieces or cut all measured pieces in the same direction. If you are using a commercial pattern, follow the layout guide, taking care to match stripes, plaids, and prints (page 92).

If you are cutting full fabric widths that need to match, cut the first panel and lay it on the remaining fabric, right side up. Shift the cut panel to perfectly align with the stripe, prints, or plaid on the fabric beneath it. Cut the second panel. Repeat for each of the matching panels.

For smaller square or rectangular items—pillows, placemats, table runners—mark the cutting lines directly on the fabric with measuring and marking tools or make your own pattern.

Make your own patterns for seat cushions and pillows with translucent paper, so you can easily position any design motifs.

the perfect seam

Seams are the basic construction elements that transform flat fabrics into curtains, cushions, and home fashions. Most often, you will sew a straight-stitch seam with a stitch length of 8 to 12 stitches per inch (2.5 cm). Set the machine for fewer stitches per inch when sewing heavy fabrics, more stitches per inch when sewing lightweight fabrics. For home décor sewing, the seam allowance is usually $1/2$" (1.3 cm).

Make sure your machine is threaded correctly and has a relatively new needle (the rule of thumb is, change your needle after every eight hours of sewing). The bobbin thread should be the same weight as the needle thread.

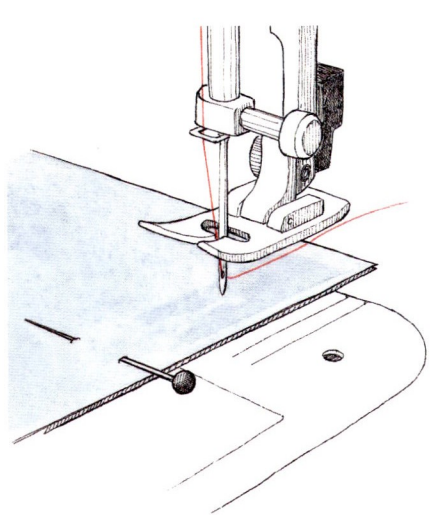

1   Pin the fabric layers with right sides together (unless otherwise noted) and raw edges even. Insert pins perpendicular to the edge about every 2" (5.1 cm), with all the heads facing in the same direction so you can remove them easily as you come to them.

2   Lift the presser foot and raise the needle to its highest position by turning the hand wheel toward you. Pull the bobbin and top threads, together, to the back of the presser foot and off to one side—to keep them from tangling as you begin to sew.

3   Position the fabric under the presser foot so the cut edges align with the $1/2$" (1.3 cm) seam allowance marking on the throat plate. The perpendicular edge should be slightly behind the presser foot.

4   Lower the presser foot. Adjust the machine setting to stitch in reverse. Backstitch to the top edges of the fabric, holding the thread tails for the first few stitches.

5   Change the machine setting to stitch forward. Stitch over the backstitches and continue stitching to the end of the seam.

6   Backstitch again for about $1/2$" (1.3 cm). Raise the presser foot and pull the fabric out from under it. If the bobbin thread does not release easily, turn the hand wheel toward you until it does. Clip the threads close to the stitching.

To pivot (turn a corner), leave the needle in the fabric, lift the presser foot, and turn the fabric. Lower the presser foot and continue stitching.

pressing pointers

Frequent and careful pressing is the key to professional-looking home décor. Pressing is not the same process as ironing. When pressing, lift and firmly place the iron—do not glide over the fabric, as when ironing.

When pressing seams, press along the stitching line to embed the stitches into the fabric. Then press open the seam, creasing the folds with the tip of the iron. Press curved seams open on a tailor's ham or seam roll.

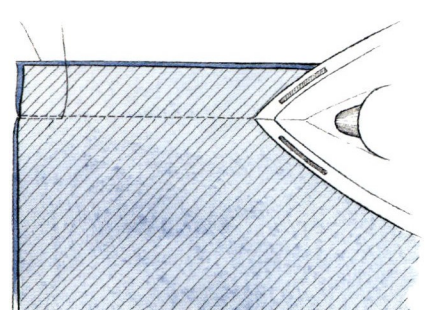

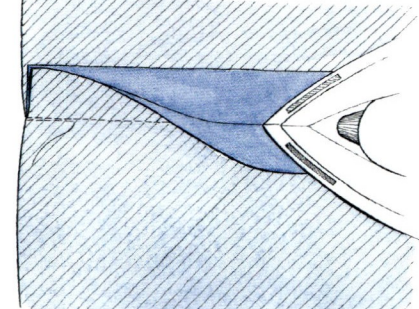

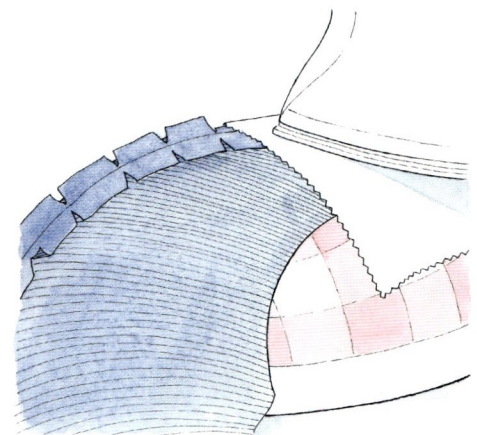

☐ Always test the heat setting on scrap fabric first to make sure the iron is the correct temperature for your fabric.

☐ Press after completing each step of the construction process.

☐ Apply steam or moisture sparingly—and always with a press cloth to prevent shine and water spotting. A scrap of muslin makes a good press cloth.

☐ If seam allowances leave an impression on right side of the fabric, insert strips of brown paper between the allowances and the item.

☐ Whenever possible, press on the wrong side of the fabric.

☐ When pressing curves, take care not to pull or stretch the fabric.

☐ Press seams before stitching another seam across them.

☐ Do not press over basting threads or pins— they might leave marks in the fabric.

check before
you sew

- [ ] Organize your sewing area. Position the sewing machine on the right side of your worktable so the bulk of the fabric can rest on the left side. Keep a wastebasket nearby or tape a small trash bag to the edge of the worktable to catch thread snips and fabric scraps.

- [ ] Make sure there is good overhead lighting and enough task lighting for close-up work.

- [ ] Gather all the necessary sewing tools and notions before you start your project. Keep sewing scissors, pins, pincushion, and seam ripper within reach.

- [ ] Set up an iron and ironing board. Keep a press cloth handy (a scrap of muslin works well).

- [ ] Wind two new bobbins with the same thread you will be using on the thread spool—in case you run out.

- [ ] Prepare the fabric by preshrinking it in the washing machine, if that is how you will launder the finished project (or steam-press the fabric if you will dry-clean the project). Be sure to press out any wrinkles or creases.

- [ ] Check that fabric grain line is straight and the cut ends are even (page 21).

- [ ] Read the instructions or pattern guide sheet from beginning to end.

- [ ] If you're following a paper pattern, press the pattern flat with a dry iron, set on low temperature. If you're working without a pattern, double-check your measurements before cutting.

- [ ] Brush the bobbin area and feed dogs to remove lint (most machines come with a small lint brush).

- [ ] Test the quality of the machine stitches on a scrap piece of your fabric and make any necessary adjustments.

- [ ] Relax and have fun!

selecting a pillow style

Pick a pillow style, shop the remnant table for a fabulous find, and voilà— you've got a quick and easy way to give your home a new look! There are basically two pillow styles, knife-edge and boxed, but there are hundreds of variations in size, shape, and decorative detail, which is what makes pillows such a versatile and inspiring home accent.

Knife-Edge Pillows

A knife-edge pillow is the simplest style of pillow to make. It is thick in the center and flatter toward the edges and is filled with a standard pillow form or loose polyester fiberfill. Most throw pillows (for a chair or sofa) are knife-edge pillows. Common variations are the flanged pillow, which has a self-fabric border, and the ruffled pillow, which has a fabric or lace ruffle around the edge.

Boxed Pillows

Boxed pillows have a foam interior that makes them firm and uniformly thick—great for seat cushions. You can cut the foam to fit the contours of a chair or sofa. Most boxed pillows are made in three pieces: a top, a bottom, and a boxing strip. The boxing strip joins the top and bottom pieces along the edges.

Another style of boxed pillow—the bolster—is a cylinder-shaped pillow, often tossed on a bed or other bedroom furniture. The round ends are sewn to a wide center cylinder and often embellished with welting (page 98) or ruffles (page 104).

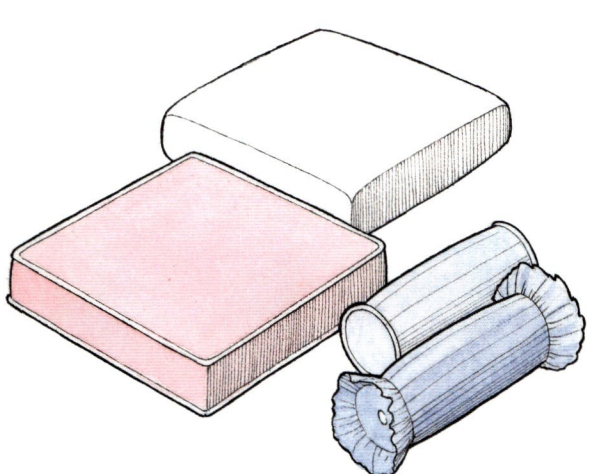

fabric choices

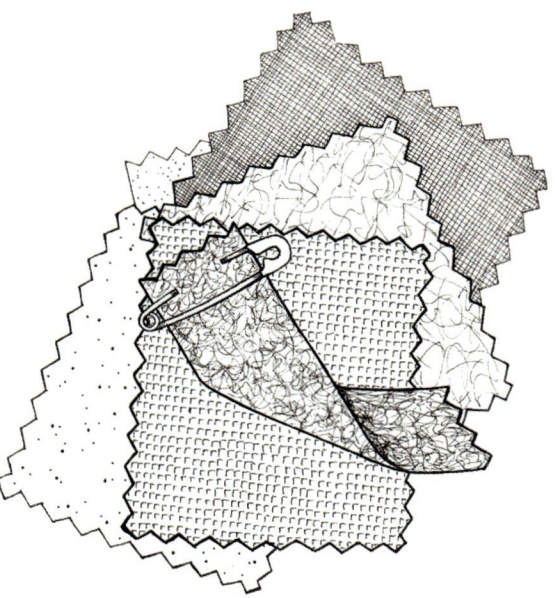

For decorative pillows, there's really no limit to your fabric choices. Be as creative as you'd like. For functional pillows, there are two important considerations: the amount of wear and tear the pillows or cushions will get and how often they will need to be laundered.

For pillows and seat cushions that will endure heavy wear, choose a durable, washable, and comfortable fabric. Closely woven fabrics retain their shape better than loose weaves and hold up better, too. Decorator fabrics are generally stronger, wider, and heavier than garment fabrics.

Popular pillow fabrics include polished cotton, antique satin, chintz, velveteen, corduroy, poplin, sailcloth, tapestry, ticking, and most microfibers (pages 18-19).

A pillow in a beautiful fabric adds charm to any room. You don't need much, so you have the perfect opportunity to splurge on slightly more expensive fabrics without blowing your budget. Shop the remnant counters and save good-size scraps from your sewing projects.

Create a lacy, decorative pillow with any loosely woven fabric. Cover the pillow form with a colored lining that will peek through the open weave.

pillow forms & fillings

The type of pillow form or filling you use determines the shape and firmness of the pillow.

down and/or feathers: encased in fabric covers of various sizes; expensive but very luxurious

polyester fiberfill: loose puffs of fiber sold by the ounce, particularly useful for odd-shaped pillows; machine washable, inexpensive, nonallergenic, does not deteriorate or mat with age

polyester fiberfill forms: polyester fiberfill encased in fabric; available as square, rectangular, and round knifed-edge inserts or bolster shapes in many sizes; inexpensive, nonallergenic, resilient

polyurethane foam: sold in sheets from 1/2" to 5" (1.3 to 12.7 cm) thick; can be cut into any shape for cushions; also available in shredded or chip form (which is difficult to work with and forms lumps)

closures

If you are making a decorative pillow that won't require washing, simply slipstitch the pillow closed. If you are making a pillow that will be laundered or dry-cleaned, you need to be able to remove the form or filling inside.

The closure can be an intentional design element—for example, an overlap closure with decorative buttons—or it can be an inconspicuous zipper hidden in a seam.

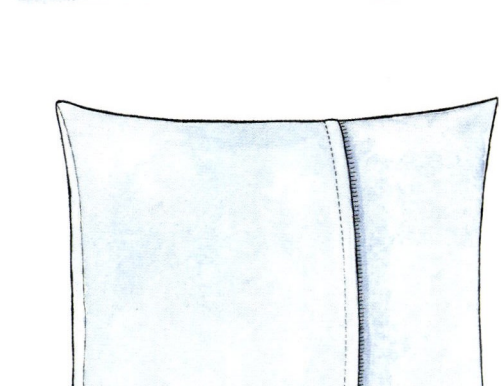

slipstitched: Leave an opening in the seam to insert the pillow form or filling. Slipstitch (page 78) the opening closed. If the pillow needs cleaning, remove the slipstitching, remove the stuffing, and clean the pillow cover. After restuffing, slipstitch to close. This method is best for decorative pillows that don't require frequent laundering.

overlap back: The pillow back is made of two separate pieces that overlap by 4" to 6" (10.2 cm to 15.2 cm). The overlap conceals the pillow form and provides an opening so you can insert and remove the pillow form easily. This style of closure is often found on bed pillow shams.

overlap with buttons: This closure is a 1" (2.5 cm) overlap closure reinforced with a series of button-holes and buttons. Add decorative touches if the closure is on the pillow front. Keep it simple if it's on the pillow back.

overlap with hook-and-loop tape: This closure is a 1" (2.5 cm) overlap closure positioned on the pillow back and reinforced with hook-and-loop tape.

zipper: To position a zipper in the middle of a boxing strip (page 34) or in the center of the pillow back, choose a centered zipper application (page 106). To insert the zipper in a seam, choose a lapped application (page 107).

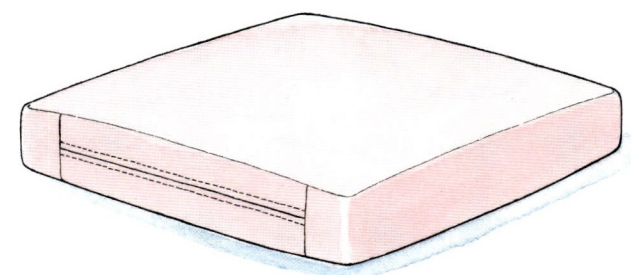

fabric requirements

Measure the pillow form to determine how much fabric you need. Use those measurements and the guidelines below to help you cut the pieces. For most pillow sizes, the pieces will fit side by side on one width of fabric. If you want an extra-plump pillow, cut the pieces to the exact measurements of the pillow form so the cover fits tightly.

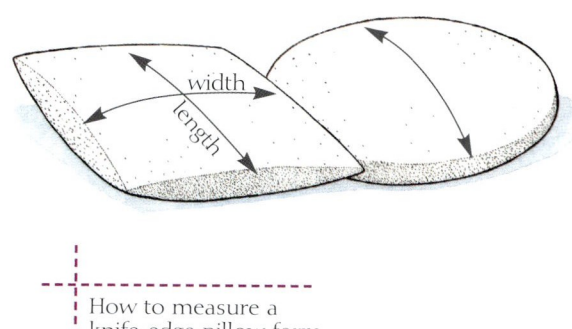

How to measure a knife-edge pillow form

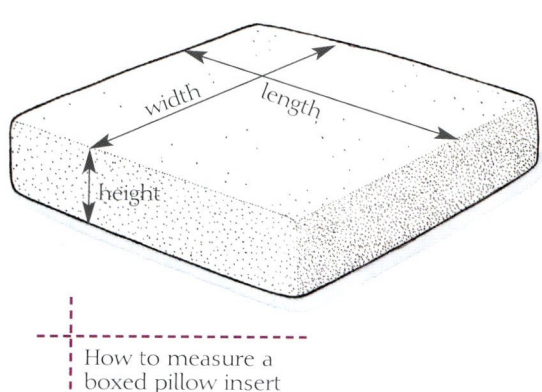

How to measure a boxed pillow insert

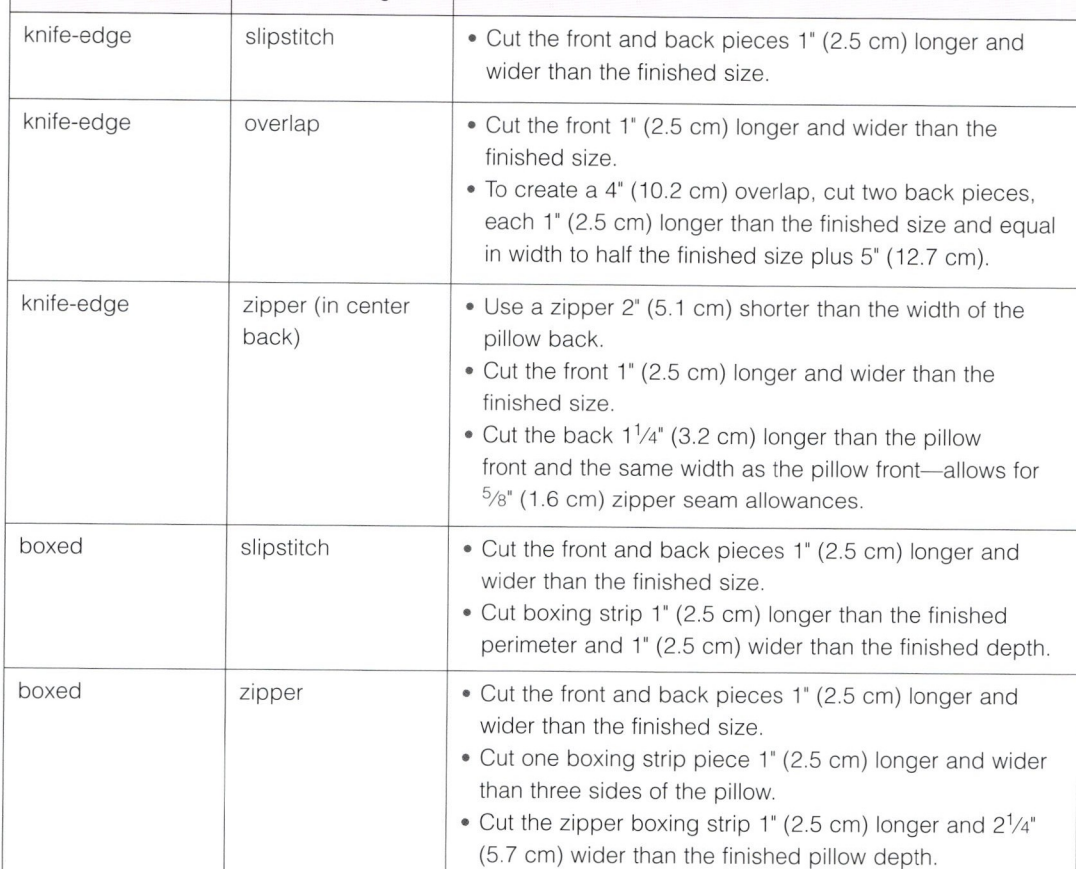

Pillow Style	Closure Style	How to Cut
knife-edge	slipstitch	• Cut the front and back pieces 1" (2.5 cm) longer and wider than the finished size.
knife-edge	overlap	• Cut the front 1" (2.5 cm) longer and wider than the finished size. • To create a 4" (10.2 cm) overlap, cut two back pieces, each 1" (2.5 cm) longer than the finished size and equal in width to half the finished size plus 5" (12.7 cm).
knife-edge	zipper (in center back)	• Use a zipper 2" (5.1 cm) shorter than the width of the pillow back. • Cut the front 1" (2.5 cm) longer and wider than the finished size. • Cut the back 1¼" (3.2 cm) longer than the pillow front and the same width as the pillow front—allows for ⅝" (1.6 cm) zipper seam allowances.
boxed	slipstitch	• Cut the front and back pieces 1" (2.5 cm) longer and wider than the finished size. • Cut boxing strip 1" (2.5 cm) longer than the finished perimeter and 1" (2.5 cm) wider than the finished depth.
boxed	zipper	• Cut the front and back pieces 1" (2.5 cm) longer and wider than the finished size. • Cut one boxing strip piece 1" (2.5 cm) longer and wider than three sides of the pillow. • Cut the zipper boxing strip 1" (2.5 cm) longer and 2¼" (5.7 cm) wider than the finished pillow depth.

sewing a knife-edge pillow

The basic knife-edge pillow with a slipstitched opening is one of the easiest pillows to make. This style is best for decorative pillows that won't need frequent cleaning. Follow the same directions if you want to make your own pillow forms, too.

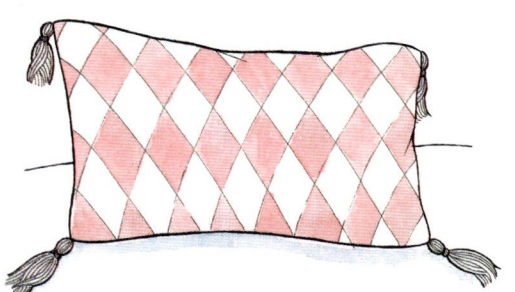

Shape the Corners

To eliminate floppy corners on your pillow, round or taper them before sewing. To round the corners, fold the fabric in quarters and mark a new stitching line, using a plate as a guide. To taper the corners, make marks on each side, ½" (1.3 cm) and 4" (10.7 cm) from each corner. Connect the lines and trim off the tapered slivers of fabric. Shape the corners as desired (page 31).

If you plan to sew tassels onto the pillow corner (page 17), keep the corners square.

Slipstitched Closure

1 Cut the pillow front and back pieces, following the guidelines. Reshape the corners as desired.

2 Pin the front and back right sides together. Stitch a ½" (1.3 cm) seam around the outer edge, leaving an opening on one side that is large enough to insert the filling or pillow form.

3 If the fabric is bulky, trim the corners diagonally. Press the seam flat to embed the stitches. Turn the pillow cover right side out.

4 Insert the pillow form or fiberfill. Finger-press the seam allowances of the opening to the inside. Slipstitch (page 78) the opening closed.

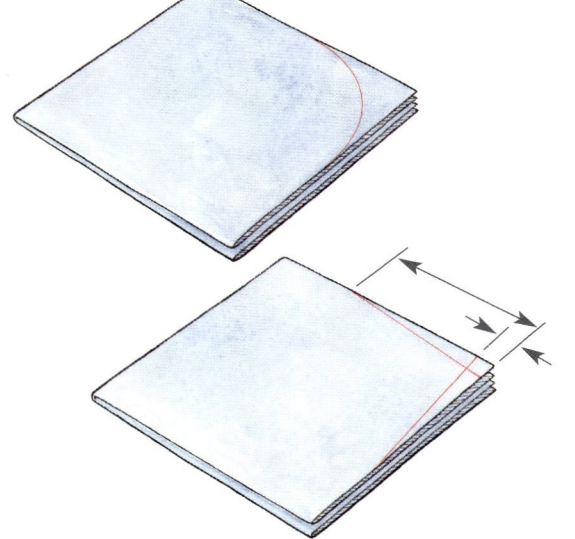

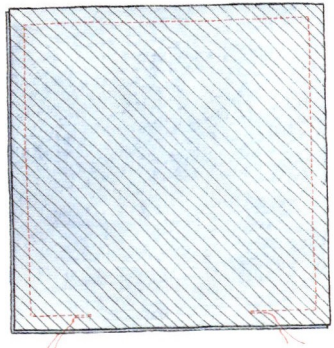

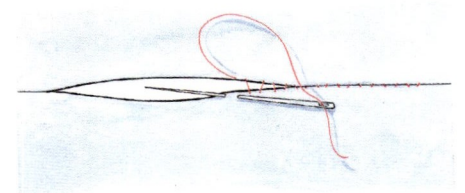

If you are making a knife-edge pillow that will need to be washed or dry-cleaned occasionally, make a cover with an overlap closure or a zipper.

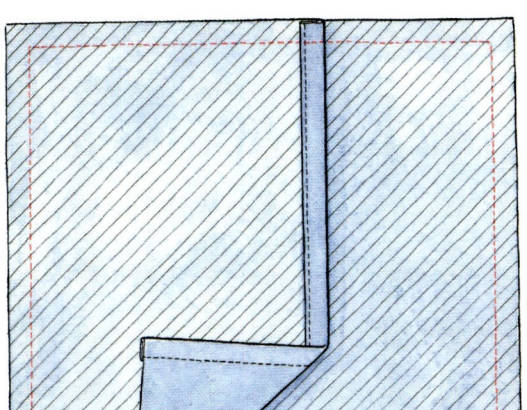

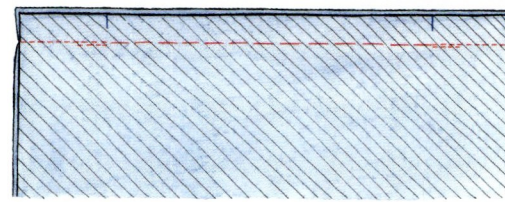

Overlap Closure

1. Cut the pillow front and two back pieces, following the guidelines on page 30.

2. Turn under 1/2" (1.3 cm) along the length of one back piece. Press. Turn under 1/2" (1.3 cm) again and press. Stitch close to the inner fold, forming a double-fold hem. Repeat for one edge of the other back piece.

3. Lay the pillow front right side up. Place one back piece on top, right sides together and cut edges even. Place the second back piece on top so the cut edges are even and the hemmed edges overlap. Pin the outer edges together.

4. Stitch a 1/2" (1.3 cm) seam around the outer edge. Trim corners diagonally. Turn the pillow cover right side out.

5. Add buttonholes and buttons, if desired (pages 109-110). Insert the pillow form.

Zipper Closure

1. Cut the pillow front and back pieces, following the guidelines on page 30.

2. Fold the pillow back in half across the longer direction, right sides together. Cut on the fold and then pin the pieces together along the cut edges.

3. Lay the zipper over the fabric and mark the ends of the zipper coil on the fabric. Stitch a 5/8" (1.6 cm) seam so it is easier to insert the zipper. Stitch to the first marking, backstitch two to three stitches, and then baste to the second marking. Backstitch two to three stitches again and then stitch to the end of the seam as shown in the bottom drawing at left. Backstitch to finish.

4. Press the seam open. Install a centered zipper within the basted area (page 106).

5. Open the zipper partway. Stitch the pillow front and back, right sides together. If the fabric is bulky, trim the corners diagonally. Turn the pillow cover right side out. Insert the pillow form.

sewing a boxed pillow

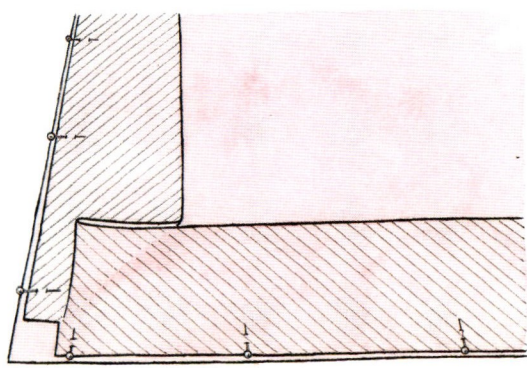

Box pillows often have welting in the seams for greater definition and stability. See pages 98-99 for instructions on making and attaching welting. You can make a bolster with these same techniques.

Slipstitch Closure

1   Cut the pillow front and back pieces, following the guidelines on page 30.

2   Baste welting (if you'd like to add it) along the seam line on the right side of the pillow top and bottom (page 99).

3   Pin the short ends of the boxing strip, right sides together, and stitch. Press open the seam.

4   Position the strip around the pillow form, with the seam in the center back. Snip to mark both sides of the strip at each corner.

5   Pin the boxing strip to the pillow top, with right sides together, raw edges even, and corner markings aligned with pillow corners.

6   Stitch a seam, shortening your stitches on either side of each corner. Take one or two diagonal stitches as you turn the corners.

7   Repeat for the pillow bottom, leaving an opening to insert the pillow form.

8   Turn the pillow cover right side out and press. Insert the pillow form, and slipstitch the opening closed (page 78).

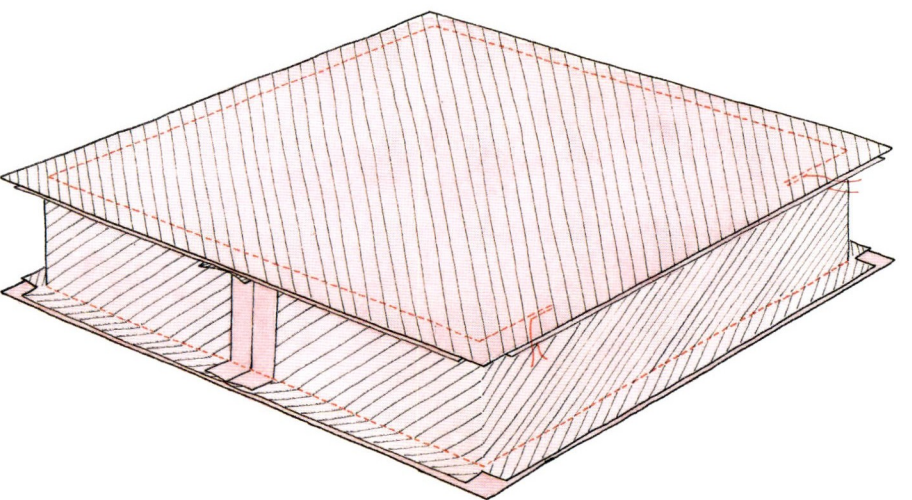

Zipper Closure

1 Cut the pillow pieces, following the guidelines on page 30. Cut the zipper boxing strip in half, matching long edges. Pin together the cut edges.

2 Center the zipper along the pinned edge and mark the ends of the zipper coil on the fabric for zipper placement.

3 Stitch a $^5/_8$" seam along the pinned edge. Stitch to the first marking, backstitch two or three stitches, and then baste to the second marking. Backstitch two or three stitches again and then stitch to the end of the seam. Backstitch. The zipper will be sewn into the basted area (page 32).

4 Press the seam open. Install a centered zipper (page 106).

5 Pin the short ends of the boxing strip to the short ends of the zippered boxing strip, right sides together. Stitch. Press open the seams.

6 Position the strip around the pillow form, with the zipper in the center of one side. Snip into the seam allowance on both sides of the boxing strip to mark each corner.

7 Baste welting (if desired) along the seam line of the pillow top and bottom (page 99).

8 Pin the boxing strip to the pillow top, with right sides together, raw edges even, and corner markings aligned with the corners of the pillow top (see top drawing on page 33). Stitch a seam, shortening your stitches on either side of the corners. Take one or two diagonal stitches as you turn the corners.

9 Open the zipper slightly and repeat step 8 for the pillow bottom piece. Turn the cover right side out through the zipper opening. Open the zipper the rest of the way and insert the pillow form through the zipper opening. Close the zipper.

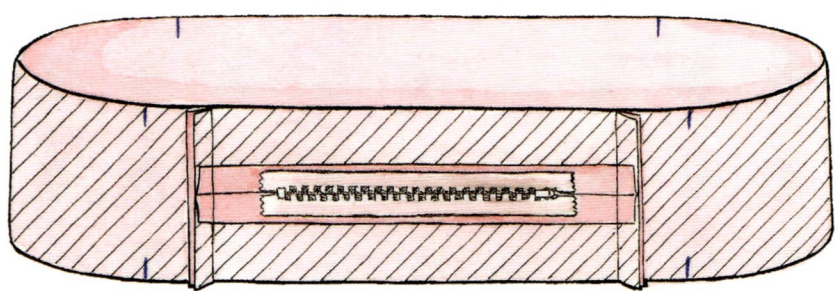

bedroom fashions & fabrics

One of the simplest rooms to redecorate is the bedroom. Start with fabulous bed linens to set the stage. Easy-care and easy-to-sew fabrics—such as polyester/cotton sheeting, sateen, and cotton flannel—are ideal for bedroom fashions.

If you are decorating a guest room, consider luxurious satin, antique linen, and lace fabrics for bed coverings. If the room has another use—as an office, for example—choose tailored bed linens. Fabrics should be durable, machine washable, and crease, wrinkle, and soil resistant.

bedspread: extends to the floor, with 12" to 15" (30.5 to 38.1 cm) of extra length to tuck under and wrap over pillows

comforter: drops 4" to 5" (10.2 to 12.7 cm) below the mattress on three sides; no additional pillow-tuck length; matched with dust ruffle and pillow shams; often reversible, with different fabrics on each side

coverlet: drops 4" to 5" (10.2 to 12.7 cm) below the mattress on three sides; 12" to 15" (30.5 to 38.1 cm) of extra length to tuck under and wrap over pillows

duvet cover: removable cover for a comforter or down duvet; matched with dust ruffle and pillow shams; easy to wash; quick, inexpensive way to redecorate a bed

dust ruffle or bed skirt: inserted between the mattress and box spring and drops to the floor; can be gathered or pleated

pillow shams: Knife-edge or flange pillow covers with decorative fronts and lapped closures at back

Try decorating with bed-sheet fabrics. They are available in coordinating patterns and colors — and are wide enough that you usually don't have to piece panels together.

measuring the bed

Mattresses have standard sizes, but the depth of the box spring and the mattress and the height of the bed frame may vary. Before you begin your project, measure the bed you have—with the sheets and blankets in place.

mattress width and length: Measure across the top of the bed from edge to edge.

mattress depth: Measure from the top edge to the bottom edge.

full drop: Measure from the top edge of the mattress to ½" (1.3 cm) above the floor.

comforter or duvet drop: Measure from the top edge of the mattress to 3" to 5" (7.6 to 12.7 cm) below the bottom edge of the mattress (length depends on personal preference).

dust ruffle: Measure from the top edge of the box spring to ½" (1.3 cm) above the floor (page 39).

Bed pillows come in standard sizes, but fullness (loft) varies, so you might want to measure each pillow to ensure the best-fitting pillow cover.

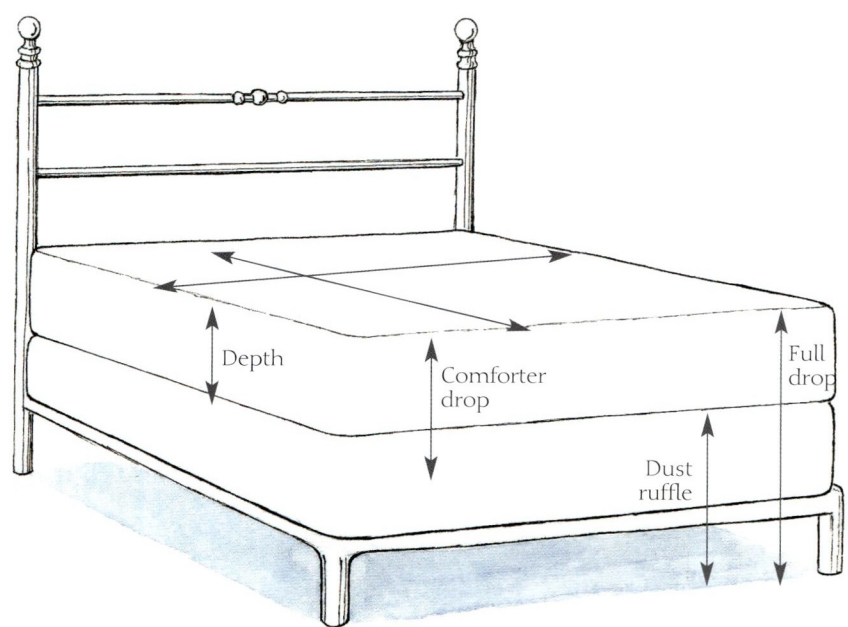

Standard Bed Pillow Sizes	
Name	**Size**
Standard	20" × 26" (50.8 × 66 cm)
Queen	20" × 30" (50.8 × 76.2 cm)
King	20" × 40" (50.8 × 101.6 cm)

fabric requirements for bed covers

Bed covers are large, so you usually need to piece fabrics—unless you work with sheeting, which is available in widths of 90" or 120" (229 or 305 cm). When piecing, try to avoid a center seam. It's much more attractive to have one wide center section with two narrower side sections (page 86).

Bedspreads and coverlets require only a top fabric. Comforter and duvet covers require a top and bottom fabric, and comforters also need a layer of batting.

The amount of fabric you need depends on the fabric width and the size of the bed covering—and on the pattern repeat, if there is one (page 86).

finished bed cover length = [bed length] + [desired drop length] + [12" to 15" (30.5 to 38.1 cm) for pillow tuck, if desired]

finished bed cover length = [bed width] + [two times desired drop length]

cut length = [finished bed cover length] + 4" (10.2 cm)

cut width = [finished bed cover width] + 4" (10.2 cm)

To determine how many widths of fabric you need, divide the cut width by the fabric width. Round up the number.

To determine the total length of fabric you need to buy, multiply the number of widths you need by the cut length.

sewing a duvet cover

1 Measure the duvet or comforter.

2 For the duvet front, add 1" (2.5 cm) to the finished width and to the finished length. For the duvet back, add 1" (2.5 cm) to the finished width and 2½" (6.4 cm) to the finished length (to accommodate the zipper).

3 Cut the front and back pieces. If you need to piece the fabric, use a full width for the center and equal partial widths for the sides. When piecing, sew the front pieces together, using ½" (1.3 cm) seam allowances. Finish the seam allowances. Repeat for the back pieces.

4 Fold 16" (40.6 cm) of the back panel at the lower edge, right sides together. Press the fold. Lay the zipper over the fold and mark both ends of the zipper. Stitch a ¾" (1.9 cm) wide seam, backstitch at the mark, and then baste to the other mark. Backstitch again and continue stitching to the end with a regular stitch length.

5 Cut the back apart on the fold. Press the seam open. Install a centered zipper (page 106).

6 Open the zipper partway. Pin the cover front to the cover back, right sides together. Trim the back to fit if necessary. Stitch around all sides with a ½" (1.3 cm) seam allowance.

7 Trim the seam allowances and corners. Finish the seam allowances together. Turn the duvet cover right side out. Press. Insert the duvet or comforter.

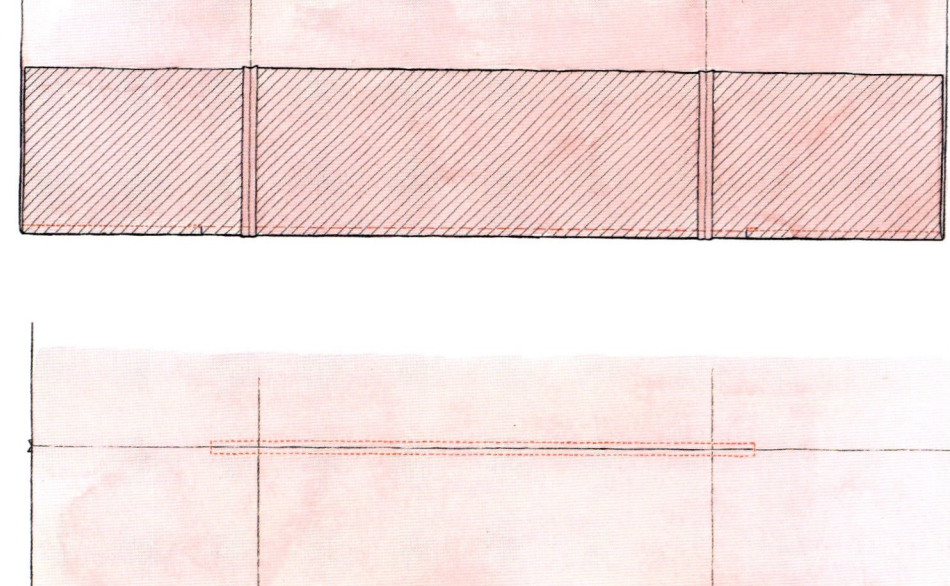

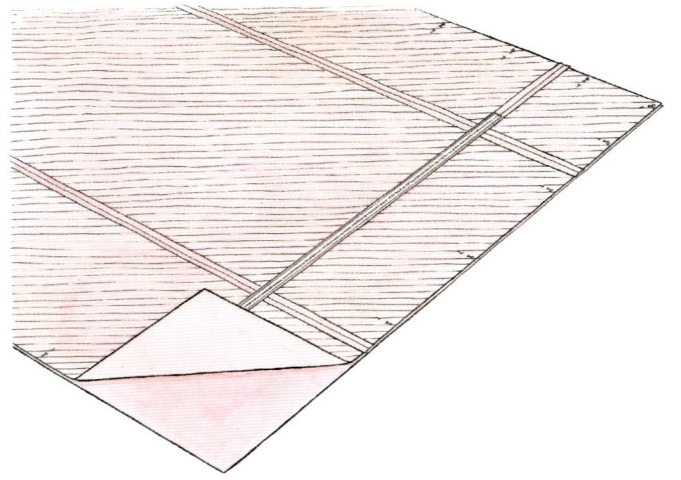

sewing a
dust ruffle

$\mathcal{D}$ust ruffles, or bed skirts, are pleated or gathered fabric panels that fall around the sides and foot of a bed. The skirt is often split at the corners to accommodate the legs of the footboard. Work with a fitted sheet or a piece of muslin to make the "deck." The dust ruffle is attached to the deck, which spans the width of the box spring.

For a gathered dust ruffle:

Cut length = [desired skirt drop] + [2½" (6.4 cm) for bottom hem and top seam allowance]

Cut width = [total measurement of two sides + measurement of foot of bed] x [2½ (for fullness)]

To determine how many panels you need to cut, divide the total skirt width (sideways) by the width of the fabric (minus selvages).

To determine the amount of fabric you need to buy, multiply the number of panels by the cut length.

1 Piece muslin as needed to make the deck (or put a fitted sheet on the box spring and mark a stitching line on the top edge with a fabric-marking pen).

2 Cut the dust ruffle pieces on the crosswise grain to save fabric. Piece as necessary to obtain desired width.

3 Hem the bottom edge and side ends of the ruffle with a 1" (2.5 cm) double-fold hem (page 111).

4 Gather the upper edge of the ruffle (page 103). Pin the dust ruffle to the sides and foot of the deck, right sides together.

5 Sew the skirt to the deck. Finish the seam allowances together.

6 Lay the deck between the mattress and box spring and arrange the ruffle around the perimeter of the bed.

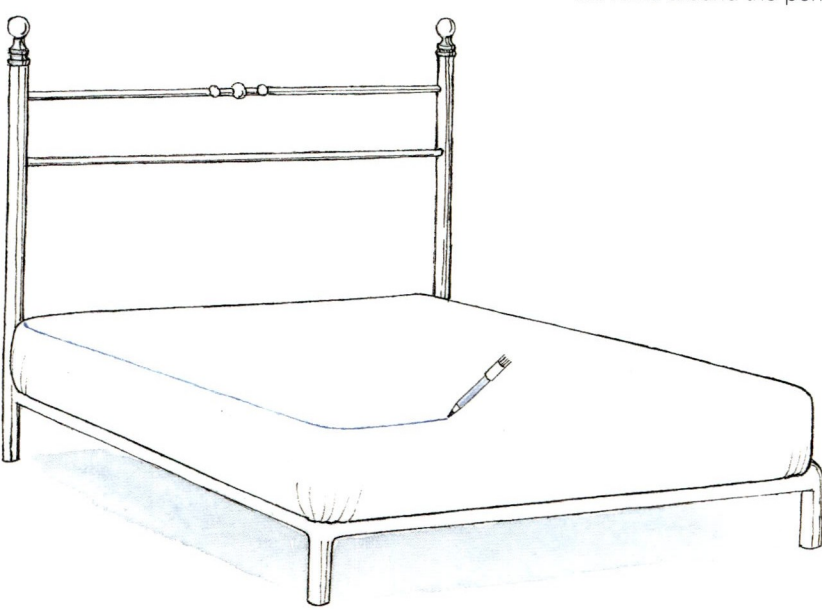

bathroom fashions & fabrics

Update your bathroom in no time with a new shower curtain and coordinating bath towels (much easier than installing new plumbing)!

You can make a simple shower curtain, with grommets or buttonholes at the top, to hang from a rod with rings. Or you can design a decorative heading—with a rod pocket (pages 71-72), tabs (page 73), or heading tapes (page 75)—to add a design twist.

Make your shower curtain with a machine-washable fabric. You might want to choose a water-repellant fabric, such as ripstop nylon. If the fabric is not water-repellant, make a plastic curtain liner from waterproof nylon or vinyl. The decorative curtain hangs outside the bathtub or shower stall, and the plastic liner hangs inside to divert water into the drain.

You can hang the curtain and liner from the same rings, as long as the holes in each heading align. Or you can add a separate, smaller tension rod for the liner. The liner should be flat and span straight across the bathtub or shower stall so that it dries efficiently. The curtain itself can be decorative, with soft folds, gathering, or pleats.

To unify the room, choose bath towels that complement or contrast with the pattern or color of your shower curtain fabric. Stitch on washable ribbons and trims to add your own personal touch (page 43).

sewing a shower curtain

First, measure the width and length of the opening for your shower stall or bathtub area. To make the shower curtain, add 8" (20.3 cm) to the length measurement and 4" (10.2 cm) to the width measurement. The extra width and length allow for 1" (2.5 cm) double-fold hems at the sides and 2" (5.1 cm) double-fold hems at the top and bottom.

If your shower or bathtub opening is not standard size—72" × 72" (182.9 × 182.9 cm)—you may also need to make your own plastic liner (make the curtain from waterproof fabric).

Measure the distance from the bottom of the rod to well below the top edge of the tub or stall (but not completely to the floor). Also measure the width of the opening from side to side. To make the liner, cut a large sheet of plastic to those dimensions or trim a standard-size liner, as needed.

Ring Holes

Your curtain and liner will hang on rings supported by a rod. The rings pass through holes in the headings of the two fabrics. You can reinforce the holes with stitched buttonholes (page 109) or grommets.

Grommets are one-piece or two-piece metal rings. They come in several sizes, with a silver or brass finish. Grommets are installed with special tools, which are sold separately. Follow the manufacturer's instructions to apply them.

1. Cut fabric for the curtain to your desired size (or piece fabrics, if necessary, for width).

2. Sew 2" (5.1 cm) double-fold hems at the sides (page 111).

3. Sew a 2" (5.1 cm) double-fold hem at the bottom.

4. Fuse a 2" (5.1 cm) wide strip of fusible interfacing to the wrong side of the top edge to stabilize and reinforce the heading for the buttonholes or grommets.

5. Sew a 2" (5.1 cm) double-fold hem at the upper edge.

6. Cut a plastic liner, if necessary, or trim a standard liner to size.

7. Lay the liner over the curtain, with the top edge ¼" (6 mm) below the top edge of the curtain. Mark hole positions by marking through the holes of the liner. If you are making your own liner, cut small holes at even intervals across the width of the liner. The holes should be placed approximately 6" (15.2 cm) apart—the first and last holes should be 3" (7.6 cm) from the finished side edge.

8. Apply grommets or make vertical buttonholes at the marks on the curtain fabric (page 109).

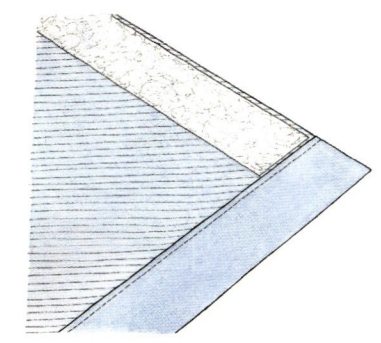

4

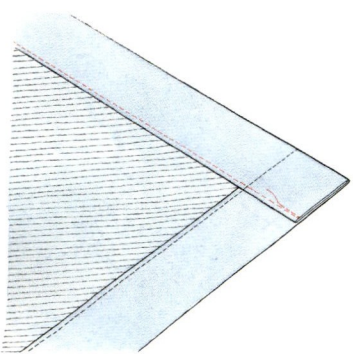

5

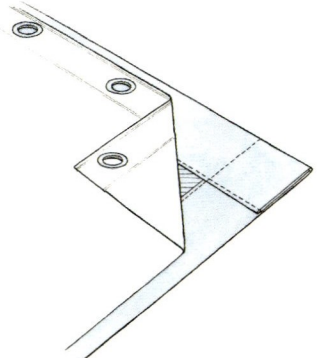

6

sewing bath towels

You have two options—and they're both easy. You can buy plain, inexpensive bath towels in the color or pattern of your choice and decorate them with laces, trims, or edgings. Or you can simply make your own towels.

Terry is the most popular bath-towel fabric. It has surface loops on both sides—or sometimes loops on one side and velour on the other. Terry is very absorbent, but tends to shrink, so prewash the fabric before sewing.

Decide on the style of towel you'd like to make. Find the standard measurements in the chart and add $\frac{1}{2}$" (1.3 cm) on each side for the hem allowance. To hem, serge or zigzag-stitch the raw edges. Then fold the edges under $\frac{1}{2}$" (1.3 cm) and topstitch along the fold.

Choose a complementary or contrasting trim. Keep the rest of your bathroom furnishings in mind as you choose colors and patterns. Glue the trim in position with fabric adhesive. Loosen the machine tension and lengthen the stitch length so the trim will lie flat on the surface of the towel.

Lap the folded or hemmed fabric edge over the edge of the trim. Topstitch the fabric to secure the trim. Or sew the trim on the right side of the fabric and cover the seam with a decorative ribbon.

Standard Towel Sizes

Style	Size
Washcloth	13" × 13" (33 × 33 cm)
Fingertip Towel	11" × 18" (27.9 × 45.7 cm)
Hand Towel	16" × 30" (40.6 × 76.2 cm)
Bath Towel	from 27" × 52" to 30" × 58" (from 68.6 × 132.1 cm to 76.2 × 147.3 cm)
Bath Sheet (a luxurious, larger size towel)	35" × 60" (88.9 × 152.4 cm)

If the toes of the presser foot get caught in the loops of terry fabric, wrap the foot with tape—or switch to a roller foot.

table fashions & fabrics

Dress up your dining room and brighten your kitchen with table linens of your own design. Tablecloths, placemats, table runners, and napkins don't require a lot of fabric, and they're quick and easy to make.

Cotton/polyester blends and medium-weight cottons with a crisp finish are perfect for everyday use. Linen and lace have a more formal look. Choose stain- and crease-resistant fabrics. Permanent-press fabrics can be machine-washed repeatedly without fading—a great benefit!

Tablecloth fabrics should have enough body to hang from the table without looking limp. Small, overall prints hide stains well (and the surface pattern doesn't require matching). If the table is small, however, be sure to keep the print small and avoid heavily napped fabrics, which can be overpowering.

Some tablecloths are wider than standard fabric widths. When necessary, piece fabrics with a French seam or serged seam, which are stronger than a standard seam. Never place the seam at the center of the tablecloth. Medium- or heavy-weight bed sheets are a good fabric source for casual tablecloths—and wide enough so they don't require piecing.

To keep outdoor tablecloths from blowing away, hand-stitch tassels, large buttons, jewelry charms, or beads as weights at the center edge of each side.

fabric requirements for tablecloths

You can sew a tablecloth to fit any size table. If your table is square, rectangular, or oval, measure its width and length. If your table is round, measure its diameter. *Drop* refers to the length of the tablecloth from the edge of the table to the hem. Place a bed sheet or an old tablecloth on the table and measure the drop to determine the desired length.

There are three standard drop lengths—each has its own look and best use:

short drop: 10" to 12" (25.4 to 30.5 cm); falls 1" to 2" (2.5 to 5.1 cm) above the chair seat; casual and perfect for everyday use

medium drop: 15" to 24" (38.1 to 61 cm); more formal

floor-length drop: 28" to 29" (71.1 to 73.7 cm); should fall 1" (2.5 cm) above the floor; for buffet and decorator tables

If you would like to add a ruffle along the lower edge of the tablecloth, subtract the desired depth of the ruffle from the drop measurement. Refer to page 49 to calculate your fabric requirements.

Refer to the chart below to determine what size to cut your tablecloth fabric. Choose the hem style that suits the weight of the fabric and the look you prefer—fine fabrics usually look better with a narrow hem (page 48).

Note that, in the calculations for the cut size of the fabric, the hem allowances are doubled—one allowance for each side of the tablecloth. Always cut the fabric on-grain (page 21).

Tablecloth Style	Hem Allowance and Style	Cut Size of Fabric
Round	$1/2$" (1.3 cm) for a $1/4$" (6 mm) double-fold	width and length = table diameter + two times the drop + 1" (2.5 cm)
Square	$1/2$" (1.3 cm) for a $1/4$" (6 mm) double-fold	width and length = table width + two times the drop + 1" (2.5 cm)
Square	$2^1/2$" (6.4 cm) for a 2" (5.1 cm) hem with $1/2$" (1.3 cm) turn-under	width and length = table width + two times the drop + 5" (12.7 cm)
Rectangular	$1/2$" (1.3 cm) for a $1/4$" (6 mm) double-fold	width = table width + two times the drop + 1" (2.5 cm) length = table length + two times the drop + 1" (2.5 cm)
Rectangular	$2^1/2$" (6.4 cm) fo a 2" (5.1 cm) hem with $1/2$" (1.3 cm) turn-under	width = table width + two times the drop + 5" (12.7 cm) length = table length + two times the drop + 5" (12.7 cm)
Oval	$1/2$" (1.3 cm) for a $1/4$" (6 mm) double-fold	width = table width + two times the drop + 1" (2.5 cm) length = table length + two times the drop + 1" (2.5 cm)

If the cut width is narrower than the usable fabric width, buy fabric equal to the cut length of the tablecloth. If the cut width is wider than the usable fabric width, you need to buy two times the cut length of the fabric and sew two pieces together to obtain the cut width.

Just to be safe, always round calculations up to the next 1/8 yard (0.15 m). Buy extra fabric if you need to match a print or plaid.

shaping tablecloths

Once you've cut (or pieced) the fabric for your tablecloth, you may need to shape the lower edge before sewing. For a round tablecloth, or one with rounded corners, fold the fabric into quarters. Pin the layers together so they don't shift.

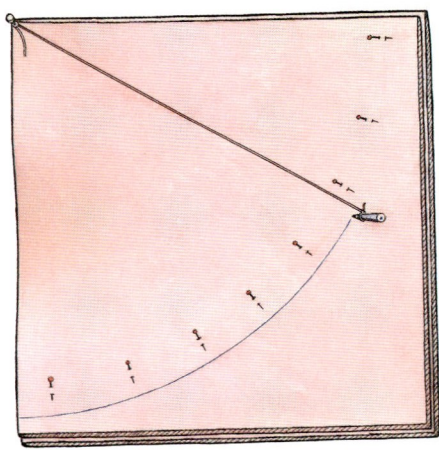

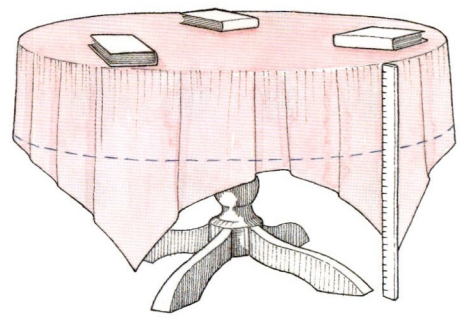

round tablecloth: Tie a piece of string around a marking pen. Cut the string so its length (from the pen) equals the radius (one-half the diameter) of the tabletop plus one drop and one hem allowance.

Pin the string end to the folded corner. Hold the string taut and mark the lower edge of the table-cloth. Cut through all layers along the marked line (or, if the fabric is heavy, mark and cut one layer at a time, using the edge of the previous layer as a guide).

square or rectangle tablecloth with round corners: Working with a marking pen and a dinner plate as a template, draw a smooth curve across the cut edges of the fabric opposite the fold. Cut along the marked line through all layers. If the fabric is heavy, cut one layer at a time, retracing the curve from each previous layer.

oval tablecloth: Center the fabric on the table and place small, heavy objects on top to keep the fabric from shifting. With a yardstick (meterstick), measure and mark the distance from the floor to the desired finished length. Mark the same measurement at regular intervals around the table. Cut the fabric 1/2" (1.3 cm) below the marked line for the hem allowance.

hemming tablecloths

After you've shaped the edges, all you to do is hem the fabric, and your tablecloth is finished! There are several choices of hem styles. Other possible edge finishes for tablecloths include decorative trim (page 17), or fringes (page 52) and bias binding (page 96). If you'd like to add a ruffle, see page 104.

Serged Rolled

A serged rolled hem is very elegant, so it's perfect for fine, lightweight fabrics. For this style of hem, you'll need a serger that can convert to make a rolled hem. Refer to your serger manual for instructions.

Narrow Double-Fold Hem

1 Stitch ½" (1.3 cm) from the raw edge.

2 Press the raw edge to the wrong side so it meets the stitching line. Press the folded edge to the wrong side, enclosing the raw edge and rolling the stitching away from the right side of the fabric. Stitch close to the inner fold.

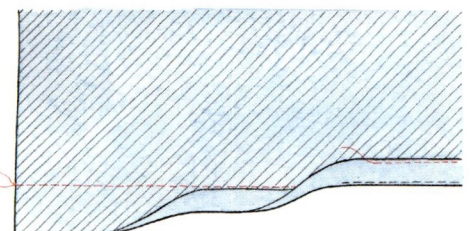

Curved Narrow Hem

1 Set the stitch length to 8 to 10 stitches per inch (2.5 cm). Stitch on the wrong side, ¼" (6 mm) from the raw edge.

2 Press the raw edge to the wrong side at the stitching line. Press the folded edge again to enclose the raw edge.

3 Gently pull the bobbin thread with a straight pin to ease the fabric fullness. Stitch close to the inner fold.

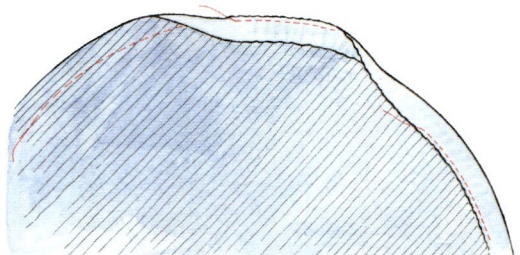

Wide Hem

1 On all sides, press under ½" (1.3 cm) and then another 2" (5.1 cm).

2 Miter all four corners (page 93). Stitch along the inner fold.

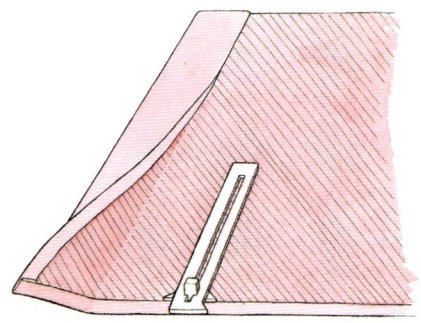

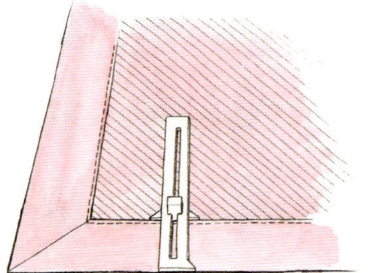

sewing a ruffled tablecloth

If you'd like to add a ruffle to the bottom edge of the tablecloth, first you'll need to determine how much fabric you'll need for the ruffle. You can create the ruffle with a fabric in a matching or complementary print or color. First decide on the size and style of tablecloth you would like to make (page 46).

1   Multiply the circumference or perimeter of the tablecloth (at the lower edge) by $2\frac{1}{2}$ to allow for fabric fullness. This measurement is the total width of the ruffle.

2   Add 1" (2.5 cm) to the desired length, to allow $\frac{1}{2}$" (1.3 cm) for both the seam and hem allowances. This measurement is the cut length of the ruffle pieces.

3   Divide the total width needed by the usable fabric width (excluding selvages) to determine how many pieces you need to cut.

4   Multiply the number of pieces you need by the cut length to determine how much fabric you need for the ruffle.

5   Cut the ruffle pieces on the crosswise grain and sew the short edges to form a large circle.

6   Stitch a $\frac{1}{2}$" (1.3 cm) narrow, double-fold hem (page 48) along the lower edge.

7   Gather the ruffle and sew it to the lower edge of the tablecloth (page 104).

8   Serge or zigzag-stitch the seam allowances together. Press them toward the tablecloth fabric.

sewing placemats & table runners

Placemats and table runners add a lot of personality to your dining table, buffet, or breakfast bar. You won't need much fabric, so have some fun with tapestries, decorator prints, and seasonal fabrics. Quilted fabrics are great, too, because the layers protect the surface of the table.

Most placemats are rectangular—but you can round the corners (for a round table) or trim them diagonally to create an octagon. You can also round the ends of a table runner or cut them square or to a point. Shape placemats and table runners with the same techniques used for shaping tablecloths (page 47).

Increase your decorating options by making reversible placemats and table runners—simply line the main fabric with a complementary or contrasting decorator fabric. For extra body and durability, fuse a layer of interfacing to the lining. Cut table runners on the lengthwise grain to save fabric and avoid piecing. Make matching placemats with the remaining fabric.

As a finishing touch, you can hem the edges, encase them in bias binding, or add fringe, decorative stitching, or decorative trim. Be sure your trims and edgings are machine-washable, too!

Type of Item	Size
Placemats	18" × 12" and 16" × 14" (45.7 × 30.5 and 40.6 × 35.6 cm)
Table Runners	width: 12" to 18" (30.5 to 45.7 cm) length: [length of the table] + [8" to 12" (20.3 to 30.5 cm)]

Lined to the Edge

1 Cut a front and a back, each from a different decorator fabric, allowing for a 1/2" (1.3 cm) seam allowance all around.

2 Pin the pieces right sides together. Stitch a 1/2" (1.3 cm) seam around the outer edge, leaving a 5" (12.7 cm) opening for turning. Trim the seam allowances. Trim the corners diagonally.

3 Turn the placemat or runner right side out and press. Slipstitch the opening closed. Topstitch 1/4" (6 mm) from the outer edge.

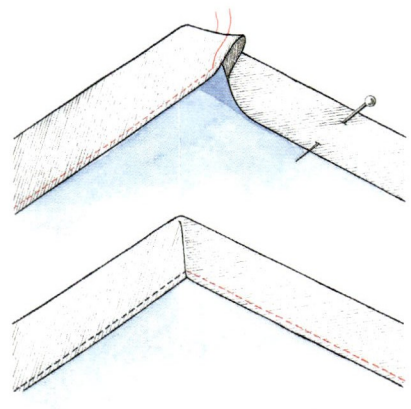

Bias Binding

1 Cut one piece of decorator fabric to the exact finished size—or cut two pieces if you are making a reversible placemat or runner.

2 Encase the outer edge in store-bought or custom-made double-fold bias tape (page 96).

3 At each corner, fold the excess binding diagonally and pin. Topstitch the adjacent side, taking care to catch the diagonal fold in the first few stitches. Repeat on all corners and sides.

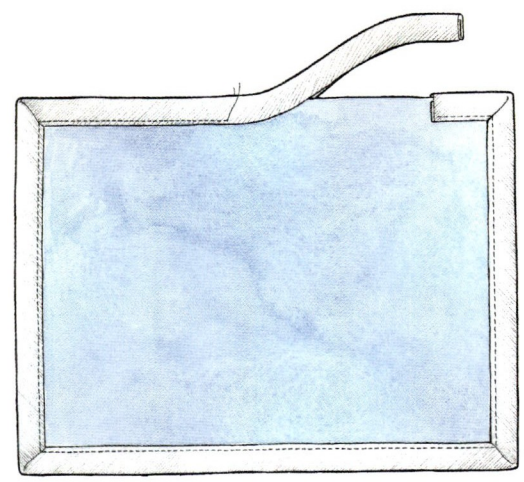

Ribbon or Flat Trim

1 Cut the placemat 1" (2.5 cm) longer and wider than the desired finished size. Press 1/2" (1.3 cm) to the right side on all sides.

2 Cut trim equal to the perimeter of the placemat plus 2" (5 cm). Extend one end 1" (2.5 cm) beyond the edge of the placemat. Pin the trim along the folded edges of the mat.

3 At the first corner, fold the trim back on itself, then fold it diagonally to form a right angle (page 94). Finger-press and pin the fold. Continue pinning and folding at each corner.

4 To finish, fold the end of the trim to form a right angle over the first corner. Finger-press and cut away excess.

5 Remove pins and stitch on the fold lines to form miters. Trim seam allowances. Lay the trim on the placemat, aligning miters at each corner. Topstitch along both edges.

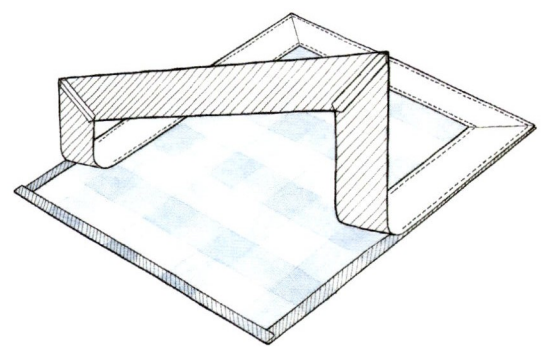

sewing napkins

Complete your custom-designed table setting with coordinating or contrasting napkins—folded simply or wrapped in a decorative ring. Choose a machine-washable fabric. Check that the grain is straight (page 21) so the napkins will be square.

Finish the edges as you would for a tablecloth, placemat, or runner—with decorative machine stitching, a serged rolled hem, a narrow double-fold hem, or fringe edges.

Napkins are typically 14" or 17" (35.6 or 43.2 cm) square.

Narrow Double-Fold Hem

1 Cut the napkins 1" (2.5 cm) larger in both directions than the desired finished size.

2 Follow the directions on pages 48 and 93 for making a narrow, double-fold hem with mitered corners.

Fringed Edge

1 Cut the napkins to the desired finished size. Make sure the fabric is cut on-grain (page 21).

2 Stitch 1/2" (1.3 cm) from the cut edges with short, narrow zigzag stitches. Stop stitching 1/2" (1.3 cm) from each corner, pivot, and continue the line of zigzag stitching.

3 Create fringe by pulling threads from the cut edge to the line of the stitching to create fringe. Repeat on each side. To make longer fringe, simply stitch farther from the cut edges in step 2.

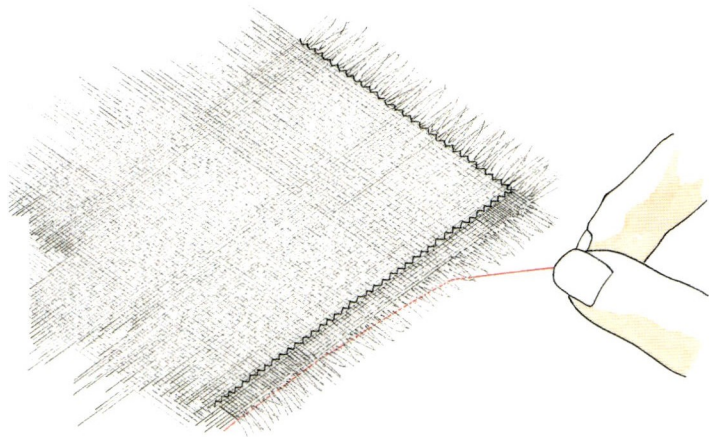

basic window treatments

Window treatments infuse a room with color, pattern, and personality. They also provide privacy, control light, conserve heat, minimize noise, and obscure or draw attention to a view.

Look through magazines, home décor catalogs, and decorating books to see what appeals to you—you'll be amazed at the possibilities. Choose the type that best suits your home (both the inside and outside) and your own personal style.

Window Treatment Style	Description	Fabric Suggestions
Curtains	• straight fabric panels that hang on the sides of the window, usually on stationary rods • usually unlined • many heading and length variations	• lightweight cottons and cotton/polyester blends; some fashion fabrics
Draperies	• long, straight fabric panels with pleated, smocked, or gathered headings • almost always lined • hang from drapery hooks, usually on traversing rods so they open and close	• medium- to heavy-weight cottons; formal fabrics, such as damask, toile, antique satin, brocade
Fabric Shades	• window covers, mounted inside or outside the window frame to filter or block light • can be flat, gathered, or pleated • raise from the bottom by pulling a cord	• firmly woven cloth for flat shades; soft, drapable fabric for gathered shades
Swags & Jabots	• swags are pleated or draped to hang across the top of the window • jabots hang down window sides and have an asymmetrical hemline • usually lined because reverse side shows	• soft, drapable fabrics, such as lace, silk, linen; choose attractive lining if fabric isn't reversible
Valances	• window toppers that hang alone or over curtains, draperies, or shades • variety of styles	• range of choices; depends on style and formality of room

formal window fashions

swags & jabots: traditionally used in formal rooms, often over sheer curtains or shades, but also used in casual rooms with appropriate fabrics

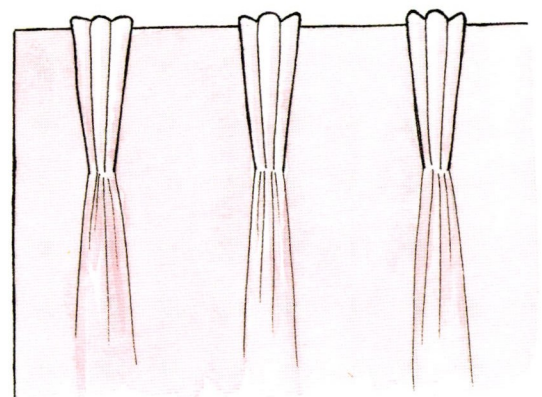

pleated draperies: suited to living rooms, dining rooms, master bedrooms; usually lined and floor-length; styles include traditional pinch pleats, goblet pleats (which pleat outward), and box pleats; smocked and shirred styles sewn with special heading tapes (page 75).

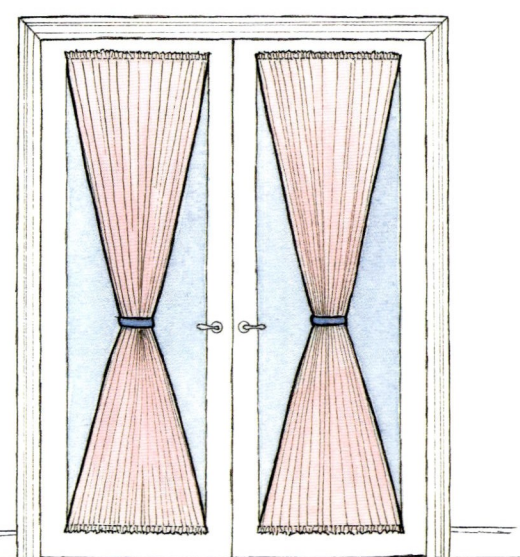

hourglass curtains: usually made of sheer fabrics for French or atrium doors.

rod-pocket curtains: formal or casual, depending on the fabric and hardware; can be floor-length, sill-length, or hung as valances

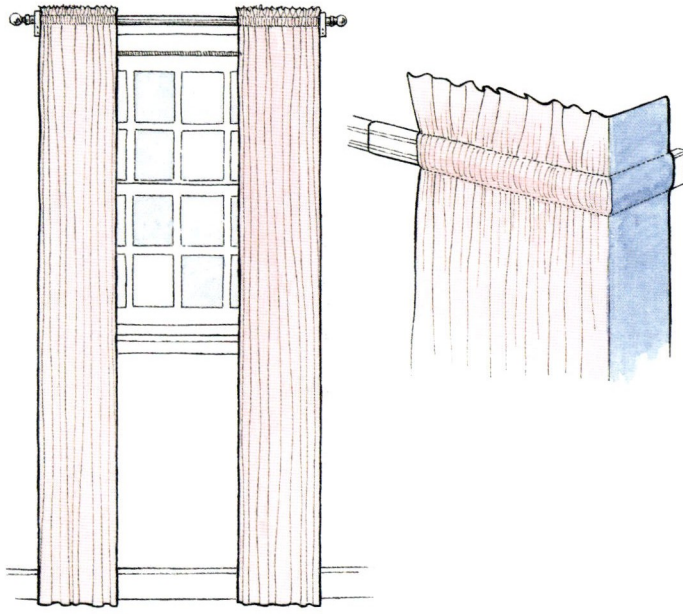

balloon shades: also called cloud shades; pleated or softy gathered panels, raised and lowered with a cord; short, stationary versions used as valances

padded cornice: upholstered box that neatly finishes the top of any style window treatment; can also be used alone

casual window fashions

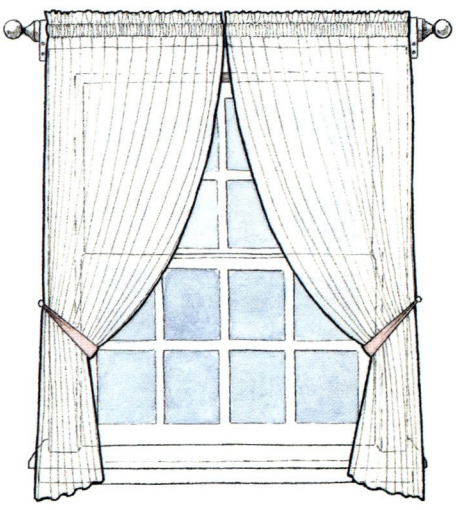
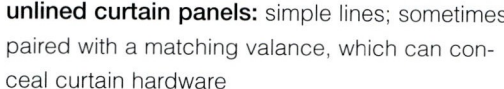

unlined curtain panels: simple lines; sometimes paired with a matching valance, which can conceal curtain hardware

contrast lining: helps the curtain hang smoothly, increases opacity, and adds a decorative accent

Roman shade: casual or formal, depending on the fabric; hangs straight but rises, forming soft folds, when pulled with cord

tab-top curtains: country-casual look, suitable for any room, particularly with decorative hardware

café curtains: cover the lower half of the window; perfect for the kitchen, bath, and bedroom, where privacy and sunlight are important; with or without a valance

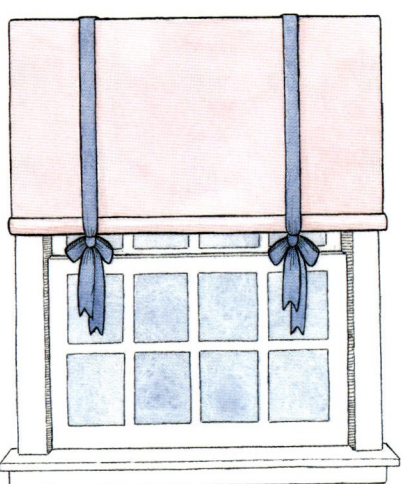

stagecoach valance: stationary, flat fabric panel with a rolled or pleated lower edge and secured with fabric or ribbon ties

roller shades: block light and provide privacy; can be made from firmly woven fabric fused to shade backing; usually topped with a valance or pelmet (a valance that hangs from a wooden mounting board)

window treatments

fabrics for window treatments

You can make great window treatments with almost any type of fabric. Decorator fabrics are more expensive than fashion fabrics, but they are usually also wider, heavier, and last longer. The average drapery lasts from eight to fifteen years, so buy the best fabric you can afford—you will certainly get your money's worth!

Lightweight and sheer fabrics are suitable for curtains, valances, balloon shades, and most gathered window treatments. Choose from batiste, dimity, dotted Swiss, eyelet, lace, lawn, marquisette, net, organdy, piqué, plissé, point d'esprit, and voile.

Lightweight fabrics (lined) and medium-weight fabrics work well for draperies, valances, Roman shades, swags and jabots, cornice and pelmet covers, tab-top curtains, and pleated curtains and draperies. Fabric choices include medium-weight cotton, linen, blends, open weaves with textured yarns, antique satin, brocade, chintz, damask, denim, moiré, poplin, satin, shantung, taffeta, and velvet.

Cotton sateen is a good choice for lining fabric. Remember to preshrink the lining fabric — and the main fabric, too — before cutting and sewing.

hardware for window treatments

The hardware that you'll use to hang the window treatment is as important as the window treatment itself. You can choose from among a variety of basic and decorative rods, hooks, rings, clips, grommets, and more. Each type of installation functions in a unique way and creates its own look, too.

Regardless of the type you choose, secure the hardware to the wall, ceiling, or window frame before you measure to determine the finished size of your window treatment and the amount of fabric you'll need.

Basic Curtain Rods

Simple, metal curtain rods work well for rod-pocket window treatments as the fabric conceals the rod. These rods are functional, not decorative. Most don't allow you to open and close the window treatment.

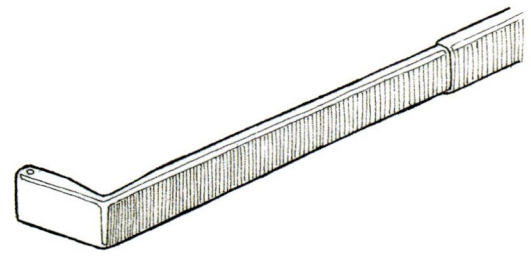

conventional, or standard, curtain rods: 1" (2.5 cm) wide in metal or clear acrylic (for sheer and lace fabrics); vary in length and in the distance they protrude from the wall; should be completely covered by the window treatment

double curtain rod brackets: hold two conventional rods (included in purchase), so you can hang a valance directly over a curtain or drapery

sash rods: flat or round rods with very shallow brackets that protrude only $1/4$" (6 mm); often used on doors or windows with sheer fabric panels

spring tension rods: positioned inside the window frame; adjust to varying widths and stay in place without brackets

traverse rods: allow window treatments to open and close with the pull of a cord; two-way traverse rod opens from the center; one-way rod opens from the side

wide, flat curtain rods: $2^1/2$" or $4^1/2$" (6.4 or 11.4 cm) wide; create a strong visual effect

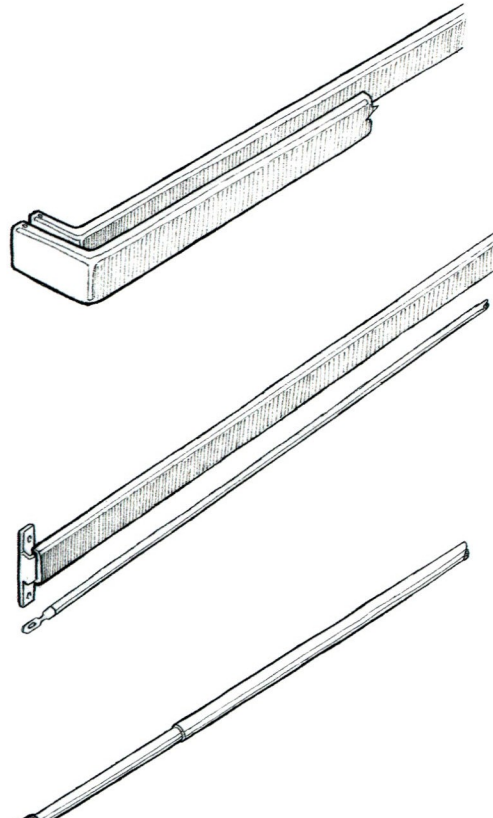

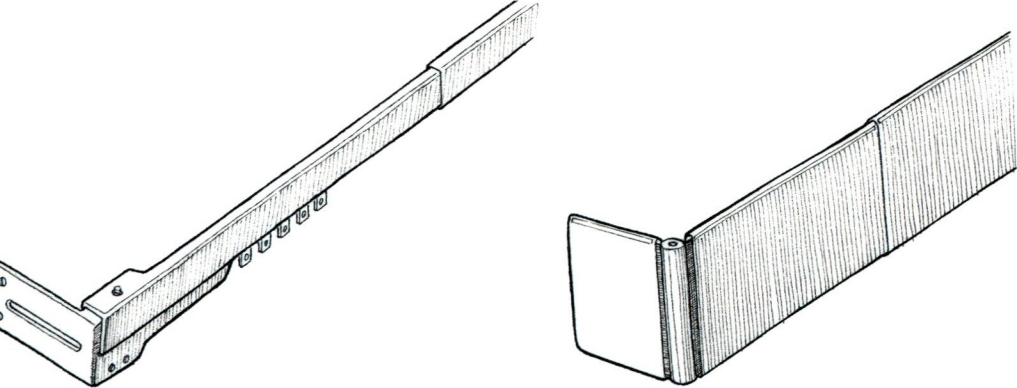

decorative hardware

Decorative curtain rods are made of metal, iron, bronze, enamel, and wood—with varying circumferences. They are often sold in kits that include brackets, finials, and rings. Many have antique or special metallic finishes, with elaborate finials at the ends. These rods are meant to be seen!

Draped swags are stationary. They hang from rods, decorative poles, mounting boards, or swag holders.

You can hang window treatments from pleat hooks, fabric tabs, ribbons, grommets, rings, and clips—depending on the look you're after.

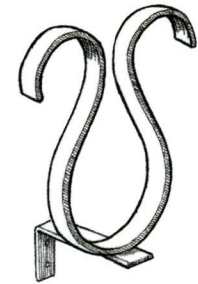

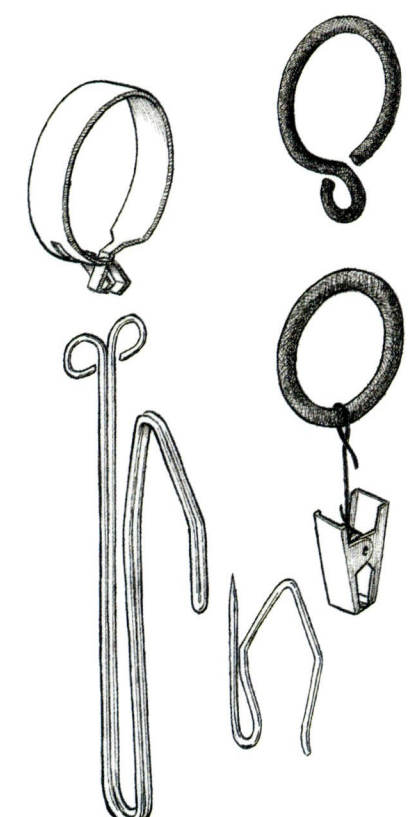

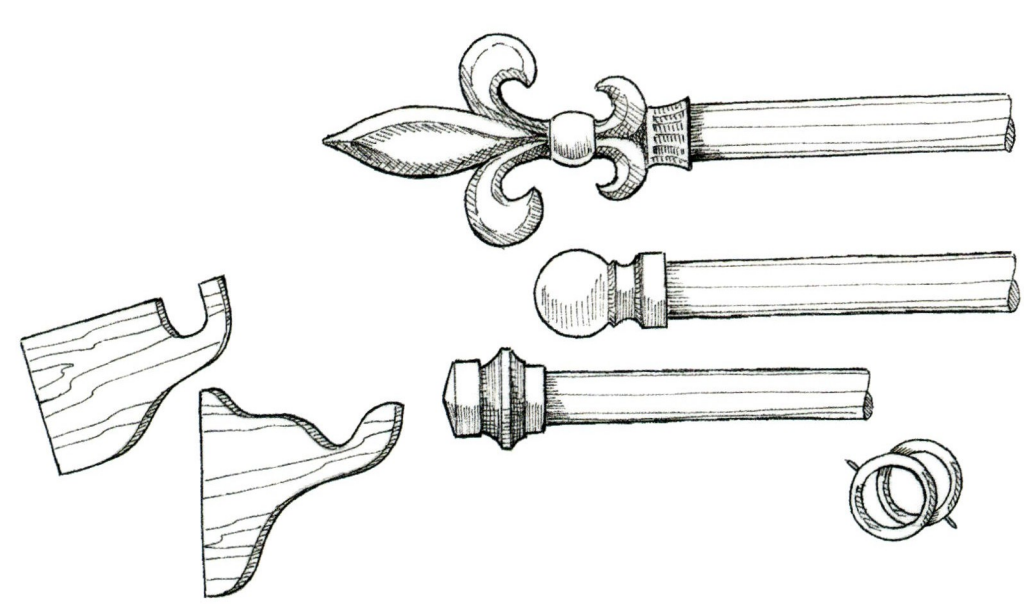

mounting boards

Instead of working with hardware, you can a hang a window treatment by stapling it to a thick piece of wood, which serves as a mounting board. The board can sit inside the window frame or outside, depending on the effect you want. Cover the board with a fabric of your choice for a professional and decorative finish.

1 Cut muslin or decorator fabric to cover the board, allowing a 1" (2.5 cm) overlap along the long edge and a 2" (5.1 cm) overlap at each short end.

2 Center the board on the wrong side of the fabric. Staple one long edge of the fabric to the board. Leave about 6" (15.2 cm) of fabric free at each end.

3 Fold under ¼" (6 mm) of the unstapled long edge. Wrap the fabric around the board and staple in place, leaving 6" (15.2 cm) of fabric free at each end.

4 Fold the unstapled fabric at each end as shown in the drawing. Finger-press to reduce bulk. Staple in place.

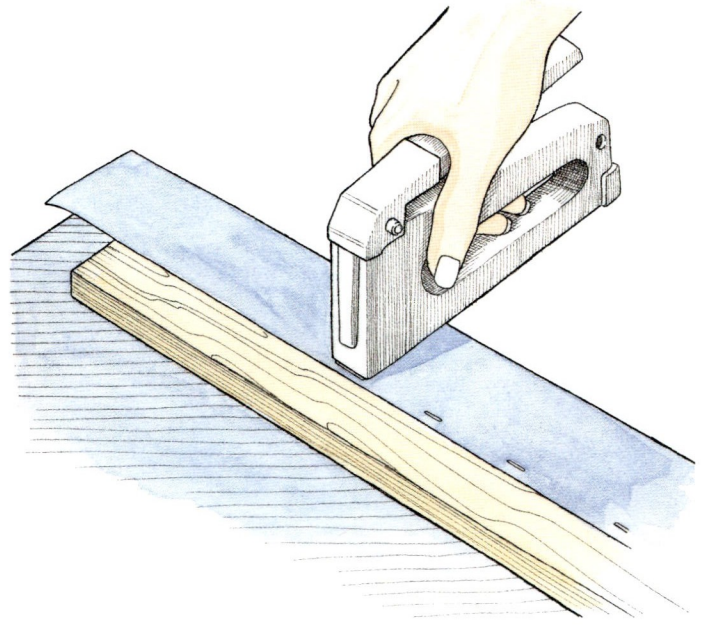
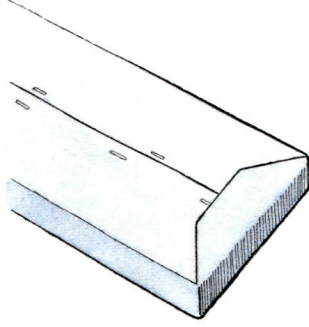

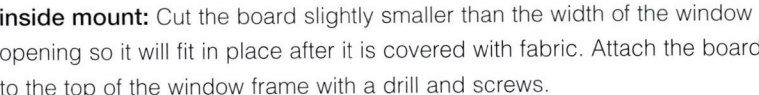

inside mount: Cut the board slightly smaller than the width of the window opening so it will fit in place after it is covered with fabric. Attach the board to the top of the window frame with a drill and screws.

outside mount: Cut the mounting board at least 2" (5.1 cm) wider than the window frame. Attach angle irons to the back edge of the board, an equal distance from each edge of the window frame. Hold the mounting board against the wall to determine the best placement.

measuring windows

To determine the finished size of your window treatments, you'll measure the hardware or the mounting board—not the window! These measurements will help you determine how much fabric you'll need.

Work with a retractable metal tape measure. If the area you're measuring is very large, you may also need to enlist the help of a friend.

Hang the hardware or board, depending on your style of window treatment.

If you are making curtains, valances, and draperies with a rod, attach the rod to the wall above and to the sides of the frame.

If you are making roller shades, attach the hardware inside the window frame or directly on the outside corner.

Cut mounting boards so they either fit inside the window frame or hang on the wall, over and beyond the frame. A spring-tension rod always goes inside the frame.

Most window treatments extend to the top of the sill, the bottom of the window apron, or 1/2" (1.3 cm) from the floor or radiator. Valances should extend at least 4" to 6" (10.2 to 15.2 cm) below the top of the window and should be 10" to 16" (25.4 to 40.6 cm) long.

Measuring Width

To determine the finished width of your window treatment, measure the curtain rod, pole, or mounting board, including the return (or projection) on each end.

Measuring Length

To determine the finished length of your window treatment, measure from the top of the hardware to the point where you want the lower edge of the window treatment to fall.

If the window treatment will hang from clips, rings, or tabs, measure from the bottom of the clips, rings, or tabs.

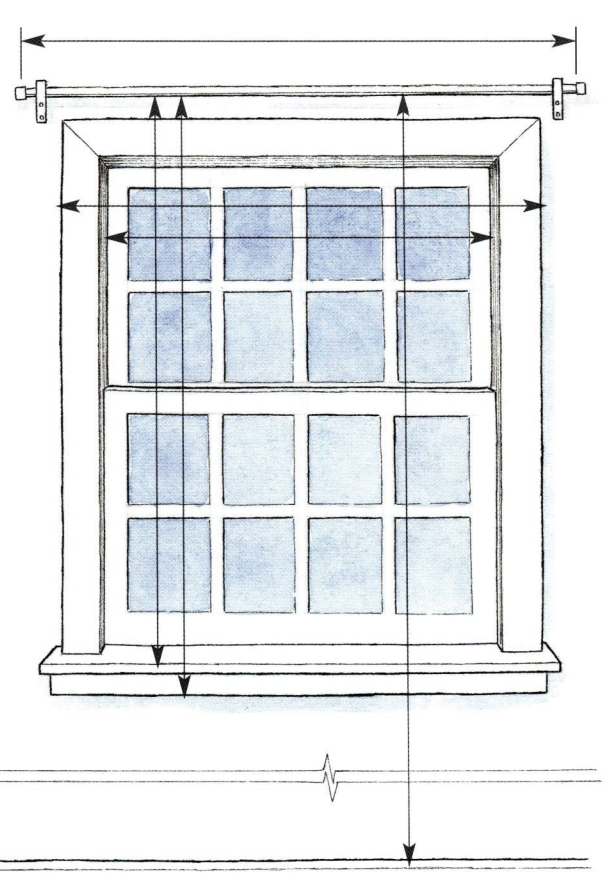

To make a window appear longer, hang the curtain rod or mounting board closer to the ceiling.

fabric requirements

The amount of fabric you'll need depends on several factors: the window treatment style, the style and size of the hardware, the surface pattern of the fabric (you may need more to match a pattern), the hemming method, and the desired fullness.

Fullness

Fullness is the amount of fabric taken up by the construction of the window treatment—usually in gathering or pleating. Fullness may require up to three times the width of the window.

The amount depends on the treatment style, the fabric weight, and your personal preference (fullness affects drape and volume). For some types of pleated window treatments, you actually need to make a paper pattern, arrange the pleat placement, and then measure the width of the pattern (page 105).

Treatment Style & Fabric	Fabric Needed for Fullness
Gathered curtains/sheer and lightweight fabrics	2½ to 3 times window width
Gathered curtains/medium- to heavy-weight fabrics	2 to 2½ times window width
Gathered curtains/heavy-weight fabrics	2 times window width
Pleated draperies	approximately 2½ times window width, depending on pleat style

Determining Width

When computing the finished width of your fabric, multiply the measurement of your window hardware by the amount of extra fabric needed for fullness.

Cut width = [finished width measurement (including returns and overlap, if applicable)] × [desired fullness] + [side hem allowances (usually 3" (7.6 cm) for each double-fold 1½" (3.8 cm) hem)]

You'll need exact cut width measurements only for flat window treatments (like shades) and those made with certain heading tapes. For other treatments, you can approximate.

Determining Length

When making window treatments, always use double-fold hems (page 111). Hem allowances vary with the weight of the fabric and style of the treatment.

Treatment Style & Fabric	Hem Allowance
lightweight fabrics	10" (25.4 cm) for a 5" (12.7 cm) double-fold hem
medium to heavy fabrics	8" (20.3 cm) for a 4" (10.2 cm) double-fold hem
short curtains and valances	4" (10.2 cm) for a 2" (5.1 cm) double-fold hem

Cut length = [finished length measurement] + [hem allowances] + [heading] + [rod pocket depth (if applicable)] + [pattern repeat allowance, if applicable (page 91)]

How Much Fabric to Buy

Divide the cut width by the usable fabric width (excluding selvages). Round up to the next whole number to determine how many fabric widths you need. Multiply this number by the cut length to find out how much yardage to buy.

sewing edge-to-edge lining

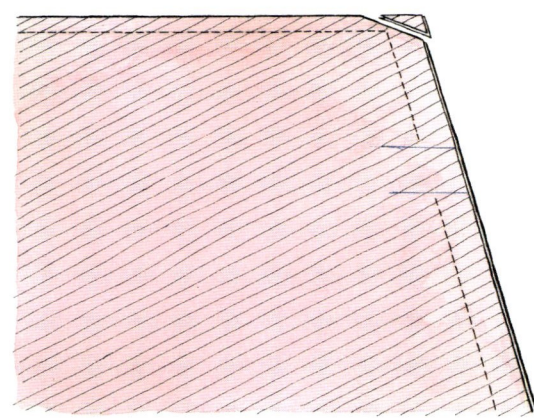

You don't always need to add a lining, but it will add weight and body to the main fabric and help the window treatment hang better. A lining also keeps the fabric from fading in sunlight, adds opacity, and presents a finished appearance to the outside world.

Edge-to-edge lining is a quick and easy way to line a short curtain or valance. There are no side hems supporting the shape, so this construction is not recommended for full-length curtains. If the curtain or valance will hang from clips, eliminate the rod-pocket opening.

1 Cut the fabric and lining to the same size, piecing if necessary. Determine the fabric amount, following the guidelines on pages 66-67—but when computing the cut width, allow only 1/2" (1.3 cm) for each side seam allowance.

2 Hem the lower edges of the curtain and lining with double-fold hems (page 111).

3 Place the curtain and lining right sides together. Pin along the sides and top. Mark the rod-pocket opening with a fabric-marking pen.

4 Sew 1/2" (1.3 cm) seams along the sides and top, breaking the stitching at the marks to leave an opening for the rod pocket. Trim the corners diagonally.

5 Turn the curtain or valance right side out and press.

6 Stitch along the top and bottom of the rod pocket, using a seam guide or a strip of tape on the machine bed to keep the line of stitching even.

7 Insert the curtain rod.

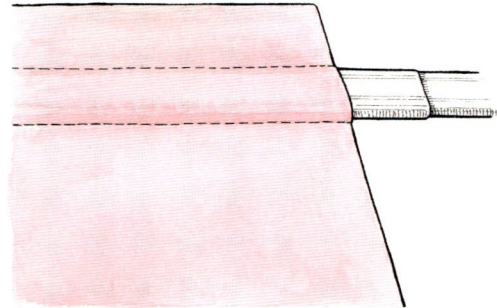

sewing interior lining

Traditionally, lining is cut slightly smaller than the decorator fabric so the lining fabric is not visible at the sides of the curtain. This lining method works well for lightweight curtains that hang from clips or sew-on rings.

1 Cut the curtain fabric to the desired size.

Cut length = [finished length] + [4½" (11.4 cm) (2½" [6.4 cm] for the heading and 2" [5.1 cm] for the double-fold hem)].

Cut width = [finished width] × [desired fullness] + [1" [2.5 cm] (for ½" [1.3 cm] seam allowance on each side)]

2 Cut the lining fabric 2" (5.1 cm) shorter and 6" (15.2 cm) narrower than the width of the curtain fabric. Piece curtain and lining panels as necessary (page 86).

3 Hem the lower edges of the curtain and lining panels with 2" (5.1 cm) double-fold hems (page 111). If you are making floor-length curtains, hand-tack a drapery weight in the hem, within each seam allowance of the decorator fabric.

4 Pin the sides of the lining and curtain, right sides together, so that the lining hem is 1½" (3.8 cm) above the hem of the decorator fabric. Stitch the side seams with a ½" (1.3 cm) seam allowance. Press the seam allow-ances toward the decorator fabric.

3

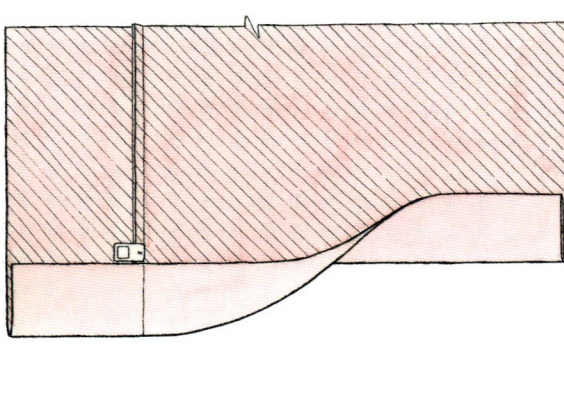

3

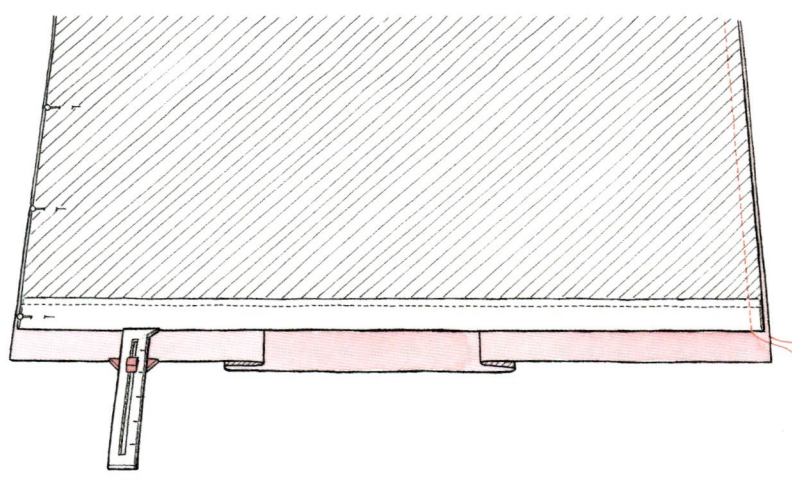

4

5   Turn the curtain right side out. Because the lining is narrower than the decorator fabric, the fabric will naturally fold to the wrong side. Center the lining so the overlapping decorator fabric is equal on each side. Press.

6   To form the heading, press ½" (1.3 cm) of the upper edge of the decorator fabric to the wrong side. Then fold over another 2" (5.1 cm), encasing the raw edge of the lining. Edgestitch along the inside fold.

7   Attach clips or sew-on rings at evenly spaced intervals across the width of the heading.

8   Fold the bottom corner of each side hem diagonally to form a 45-degree angle. Hand-stitch closed.

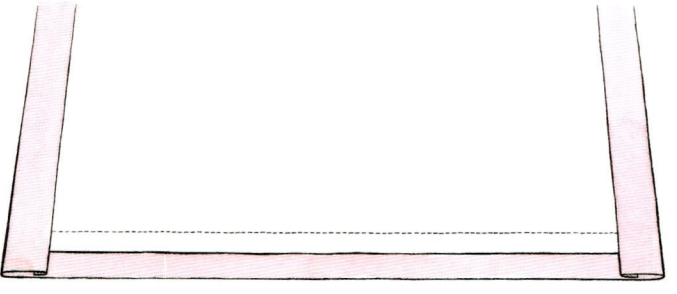

5

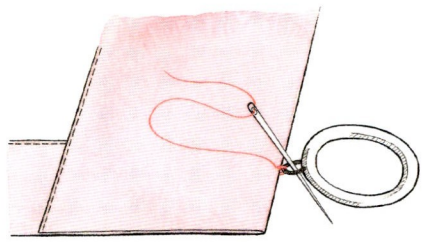

7

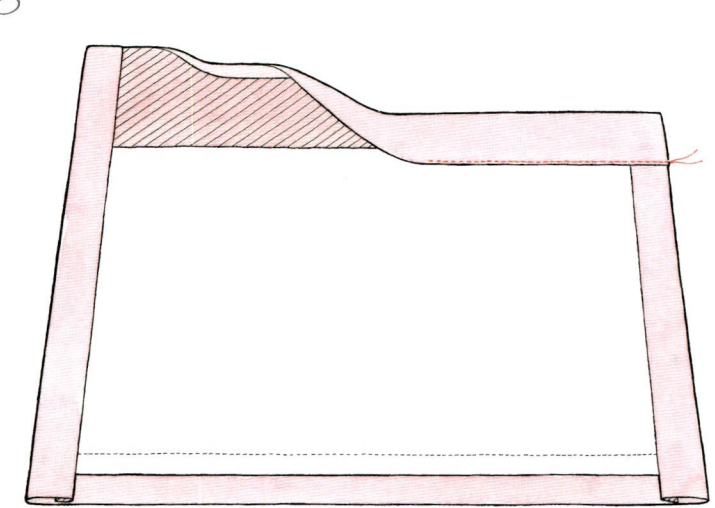

6

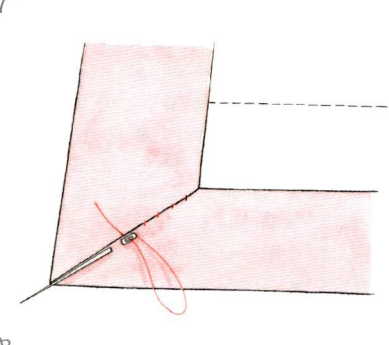

8

sewing unlined rod-pocket curtains

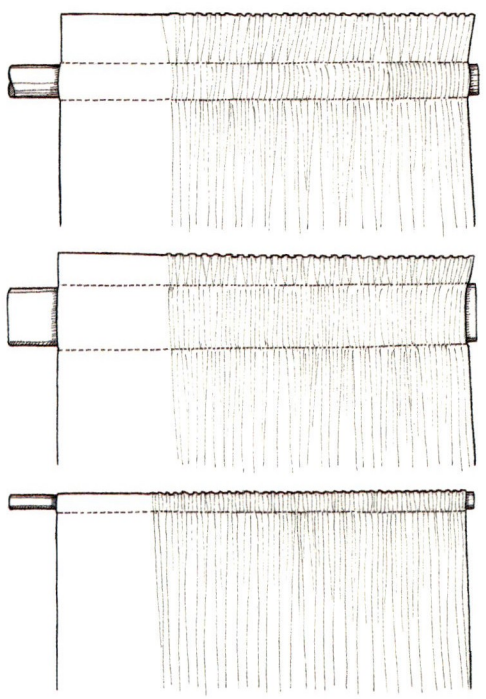

A rod pocket is a casing that holds the curtain rod or pole. Traditionally, it is stitched 1" to 4" (2.5 to 10.2 cm) below the upper edge of the curtain. The heading above the pocket forms a ruffle when the curtain is placed on the rod. For curtains used as undertreatment, eliminate the heading and position the pocket at the very top of the curtain.

The size of the rod or pole determines the depth of the rod pocket. You can use conventional metal rods (typically 1", $2\frac{1}{2}$", or 4" (2.5, 6.4, or 10.2 cm) wide) or decorative metal rods or wood poles of varying widths.

Measure the circumference of the rod and add $\frac{5}{8}$" (1.7 cm) for ease. Divide the number by two to determine the correct depth for the pocket.

1   Cut the amount of curtain fabric you need, following the guidelines on pages 66-67. Add the heading depth and the rod-pocket depth plus $\frac{1}{2}$" (1.3 cm) to determine the amount of turn-under. Piece the curtain panel as necessary.

2 Press ½" (1.3 cm) to the wrong side along the upper edge. Then press the folded edge to the wrong side for an amount equal to the rod-pocket depth plus the heading depth.

3 Stitch close to the inner fold, backstitching at both ends. Mark the heading depth across the top edge with a fabric-marking pen.

4 Stitch along the marked line to form the rod pocket, backstitching at both ends.

5 Insert the curtain rod into the pocket.

To eliminate the heading, follow the same directions, but make these changes: Don't add the heading allowance in step 1. In step 2, turn the folded edge down only the amount of the rod-pocket depth. Omit step 3. Instead, stitch along the inner fold and, if desired, stitch again close to the upper edge to form a sharp crease.

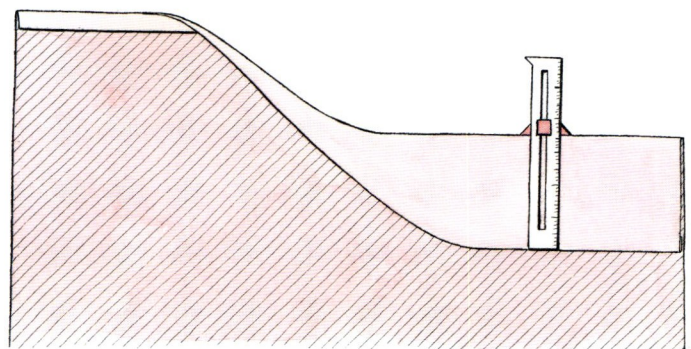

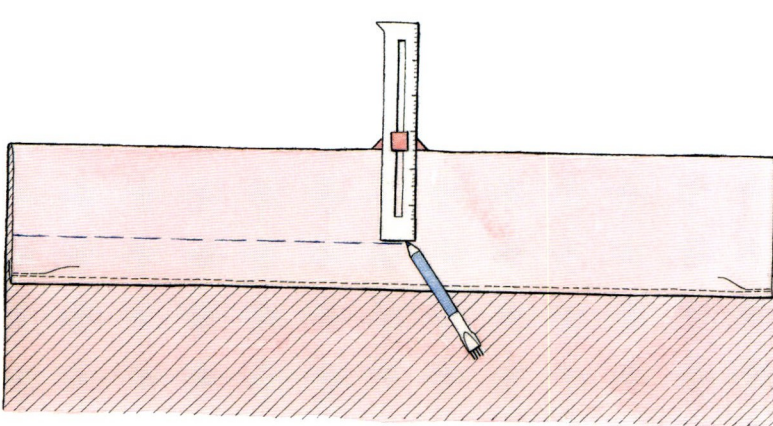

making tabs

Tabs add a nice touch to the upper edge of casual curtains, as attractive alternatives to pleated and gathered edgings. Select a decorative curtain rod or pole to show them off. For the tabs, choose a fabric that matches or contrasts with the curtain fabric—or find a decorative ribbon or sturdy trim. Cut the curtain fabric width adding 1½ to 2 times fullness (page 66).

Tabs are inserted between the top edge of the curtain and a self-fabric facing. They wrap over the rod, and both ends are caught in the top seam—or one finished end can button to the curtain top for a decorative accent.

To determine tab length, cut a strip of fabric and wrap it around the rod. Mark both ends of the strip at the point where you want the top of the curtain to sit. Measure between the marks and add 1" (2.5 cm)—for a ½" (1.3 cm) seam allowance at each end—to find the cut length.

Tabs can be any width, depending on the style of the curtain, the fabric weight (wider tabs offer more support), and personal taste. To find the cut width, multiply the finished width by two and add 1" (2.5 cm) for seam allowances.

As a variation, you can also sew strips of fabric or ribbon into the top seam—just as you would the tabs—and tie the loose ends around the curtain rod. There are many other decorative treatments for curtain headings, too—for example, you can simple weave a heavy hemp cording through metal grommets, page 42.

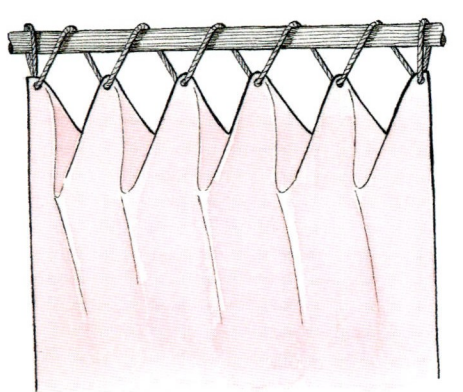  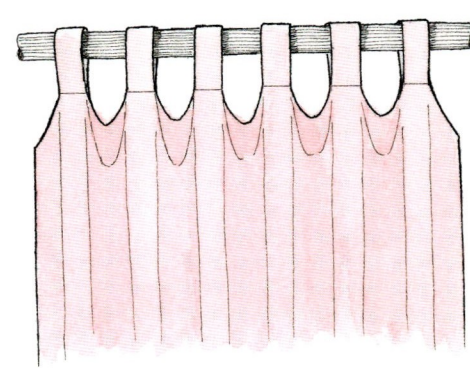

sewing tab curtains

2

1   Cut the amount of curtain fabric you need, following the guidelines on pages 66-67. Also cut a facing strip 6" (15.2 cm) long and the same cut width as the curtain. Sew a 1/4" (6 mm) double-fold hem in the lower edge of the facing (page 111).

2   Decide how many tabs you need. Plan one at each end of the curtain top, allowing 1/2" (1.3 cm) seam allowance. Divide the remaining width by the finished width of the tab and the desired space between tabs. Space the tabs 5" to 6" (12.7 to 15.2 cm) apart for short curtains; 8" to 10" (20.3 to 25.4 cm) apart for long curtains. Mark the tab placements on the upper edge of the curtain.

3   You will cut the tabs with their length on the lengthwise grain of the fabric. Cut several fabric strips, each long enough for three or four tabs and wide enough for one.

4   Fold each strip in half, right sides together. Stitch with a 1/2" (1.3 cm) seam allowance to form a tube. Center the seam and press open. Turn the tube right side out.

5   Cut each long tube into three or four tabs to the length you need.

6   Fold the tabs in half, wrong sides together. Pin them to the right side of the curtain top at the marks, with raw edges even. Pin the facing to the curtain top, right sides together, sandwiching the tabs between the layers. Stitch 1/2" (1.3 cm) from the top edge.

7   Turn the curtain right side out and press. Hem the sides of the curtain.

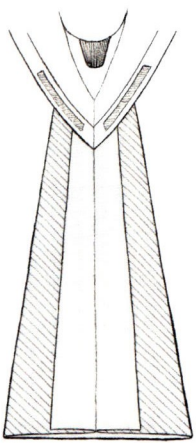

4

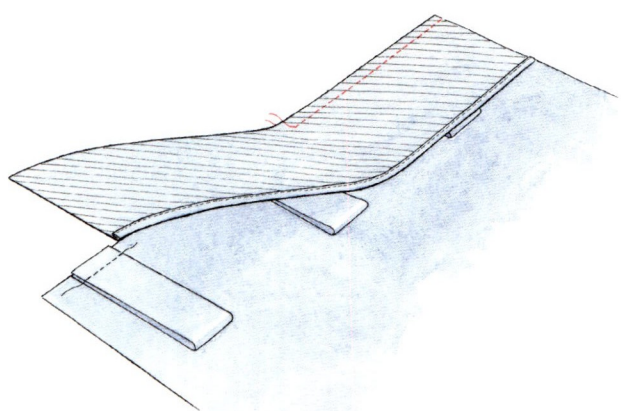

6

heading tapes

Heading tapes add custom detail to plain curtain panels. The tapes have woven-in cords that are pulled to draw the fabric fullness (page 66) into pleats, gathers, or folds. The tapes, which are either sewn or fused, work best on lightweight to medium-weight decorator fabrics.

Most tapes require a flat curtain panel that is 2½ times the finished width for fullness—but to be sure, check the manufacturer's information on the packaging. The tapes are sewn to the wrong side of the upper edge of the curtain panel (pages 76-77).

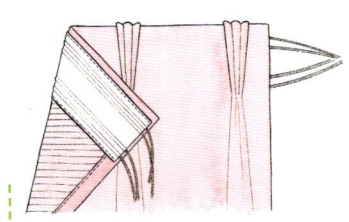

pinch-pleat tape

evenly spaced groups of three pleats; for long or short curtains and draperies or valances

fullness: 2½ to 3

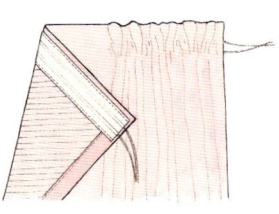

shirring tape

narrow tape that forms soft gathers; for short panels or undercurtains

fullness: 2 to 2½

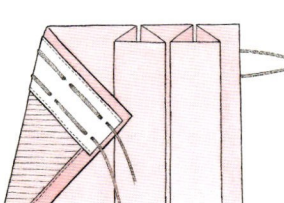

box-pleat tape

tailored box pleats; for valances and curtains that don't open or close

fullness: 3

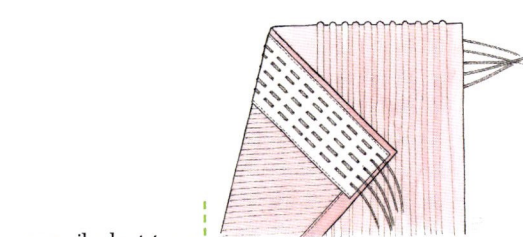

pencil-pleat tape

long, continuous, narrow pleats; the wider the heading, the longer the curtain should be

fullness: 2½

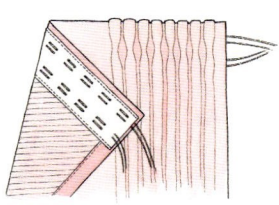

smocking tape

wide, decorative heading that resembles hand-smocking; for long, elegant draperies

fullness: 2½

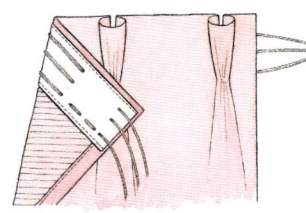

goblet-pleat tape

evenly spaced pinch-pleats that are open at the top; for long draperies; goblet pleats in soft fabrics might require stuffing to maintain shape

fullness: 2 to 2½

attaching heading tapes

When making curtains with heading tapes, you need to plan ahead. Measure the rod to determine the finished width of the panel. If the curtain or drapery will open, divide the finished width by two, allowing for a center overlap and corner returns (the amount the rod projects from the wall), if applicable.

Fabric Requirements

Each style of heading tape requires a specific amount of fullness in the curtain or drapery (page 66). Most tapes require the cut fabric to be 2½ to 3 times wider than the finished width of the curtain or drapery.

Cut width = [finished width measurement (including returns and overlap, if applicable)] × [fullness required by the tape] + [side hem allowances (usually 3" (7.6 cm) for each double-fold 1½" (3.8 cm) hem)]

On medium- to heavy-weight fabrics, add enough length to finish the top of the panel with a 1" (2.5 cm) fold to provide a flat, stable surface for the heading tape. For lightweight fabrics, cut your fabric to allow 4" (10.2 cm) for a 2" (5.1 cm) double-fold hem for greater stability. (For a clean, crisp edge, edgestitch along the fold. See page 79.)

Cut length = [finished length measurement]+ [lower hem allowance] + [top hem allowance] + [pattern repeat allowance, if applicable]

If your fabric has a pattern repeat, add enough fabric length for one extra, full repeat for matching.

Attaching the Tapes

1 Cut and piece fabric for desired width. Sew double-fold hems at the bottom and sides. The panel should now measure the finished width times the fullness required by the tape.

2 Fold under the upper edge 1" (2.5 cm) and press.

3 Cut the heading tape several inches longer than the panel width. Position the tape, right side up on the wrong side of the panel, 1/2" (1.3 cm) below the upper edge, covering the raw edge of the fabric.

If you are attaching pinch-pleat or goblet-pleat tape to a curtain with returns, adjust the position of the tape so the first pleat at each end will fall at the corner of the rod.

4 Turn under the ends of the tape so they are even with the edge of the curtain. Pin the tape in place. Pull out the cords at the folds with a pin. Knot the cords together at one end.

5 Stitch across the top and bottom of the tape, taking care not to catch the cords in the stitching. Backstitch at each end. If the tape is wide, stitch across the center of the tape, again being careful not to stitch over cords.

6 Check that the knot is still secure. Gently pull the cords from the other end and slide the fabric along the cords to form pleats or gathers. The panel should now measure the desired finished width.

7 Knot the cords after you have formed the last pleat or gather. Coil and loosely tie the excess cord, so you can release the cord to straighten the panel when you need to launder it. Tuck the cord into the opening between the fabric and the tape.

8 Insert drapery hooks and hang the panel.

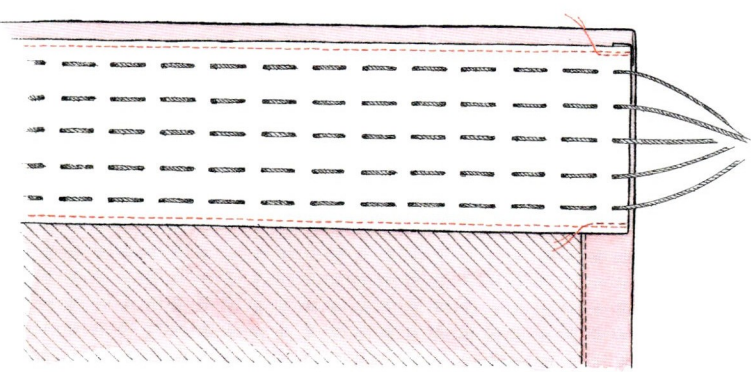

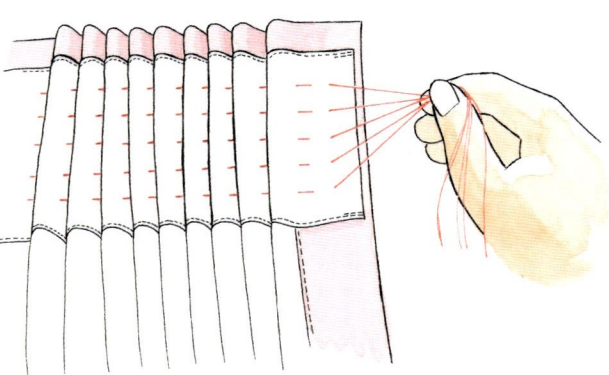

hand stitches

Most home décor sewing is done by machine, but at times, hand-sewing is quicker and more efficient—for example, when the work area is small or tight. To hand-stitch, thread a hand needle with 18" (45.7 cm) of thread. Knot one end, or if you prefer, secure the thread in the fabric with one or two small backstitches. For all stitches but the running stitch, pull the entire length of thread through the fabric with each stitch.

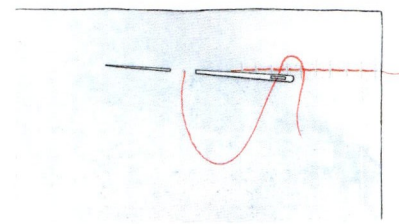

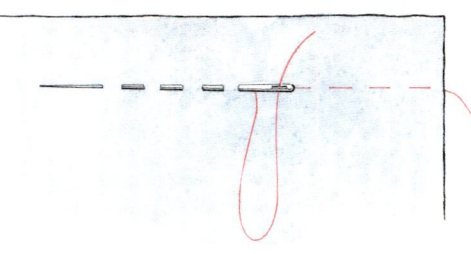

backstitch: This very strong stitch is used for seams. Bring the needle and thread to the right side of the fabric. Insert the needle 1/16" to 1/8" (1.6 to 3 mm) behind the point where the thread exited the fabric. Then bring the needle out through the fabric the same distance in front of that point. Repeat, inserting the needle into the previous exit point for each stitch.

running stitch: This stitch is used for seams. Insert the point of the needle in and out of the fabric several times, then pull the thread through to complete several stitches at one time. Keep the stitches and the intervals between them small and even.

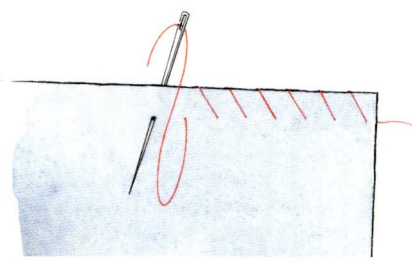

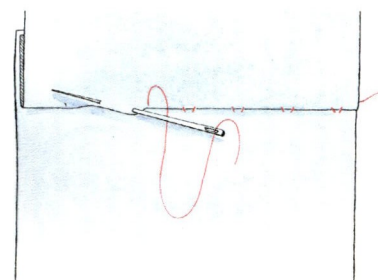

overcast stitch: This stitch is well suited for finishing edges. Form a series of close, evenly spaced, diagonal stitches 1/4" (6 mm) deep by passing the thread over and around the fabric edge.

slip stitch: This stitch is handy for hemming, closing openings, and joining folded edges. To join edges, insert the needle inside the fold and bring it out through the folded edge. Insert the needle into the fold of the opposite edge and bring it out about 1/4" (6 mm) away. Repeat, alternating from edge to edge with each stitch. To hem or close openings, alternate stitches from one fabric surface to the other.

machine stitches

Most sewing machines have a variety of built-in stitches, but you can accomplish everything you need with straight and zigzag stitches. Straight stitches form the basis for most construction techniques in home décor sewing. The zigzag is invaluable for edge-finishing and applying trim.

edgestitching: To create a sharp crease, stitch along a fold very close to the seam or finished edge. If applicable, stitch from the bottom toward the top of the home décor item.

understitching: To prevent a lining from rolling to the right side of the decorator fabric, sew and press the seam allowance toward the lining. Trim the seam allowance that is closest to the decorator fabric. From the right side, stitch through the lining and seam allowances close to the seam line.

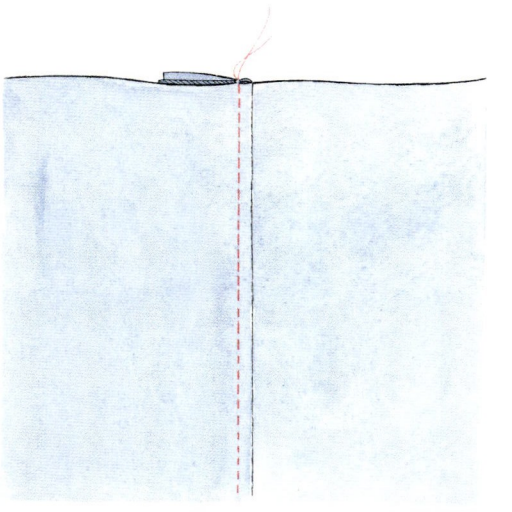

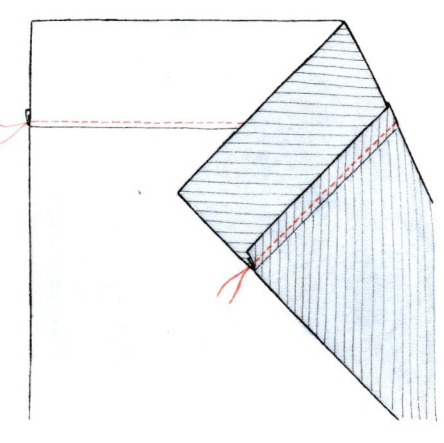

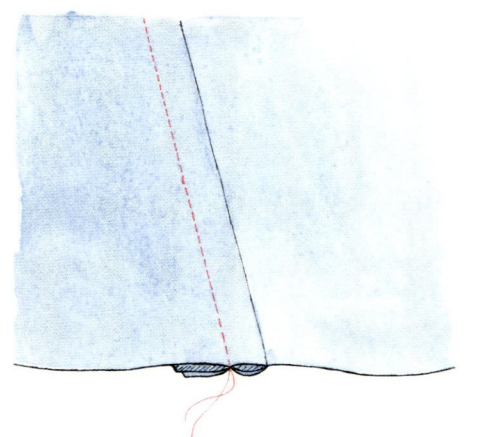

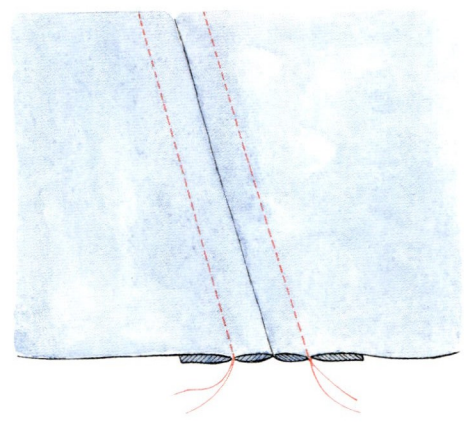

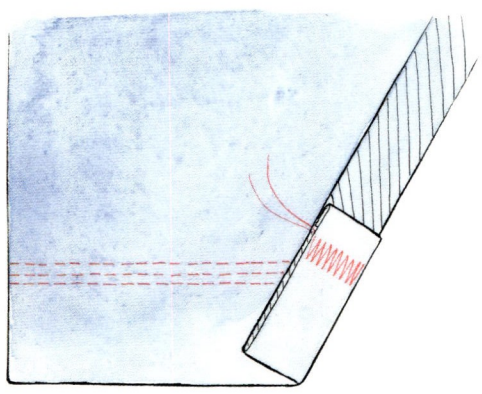

topstitching: Straight stitches are stitched on the right side of the fabric to emphasis a detail, to hold seam allowances in place, and/or to create design interest. Work with topstitching thread and a stitch length of 6 to 8 stitches per inch (2.5 cm).

single topstitched seam: Press both seam allowances toward one side of the seam. Stitch through all the layers ¼" to ⅜" (6 mm to 1 cm) from the seam, catching the seam allowances underneath.

double topstitched seam: Press the seam open. Topstitch ¼" to ⅜" (6 mm to 1 cm) from the seam line on each side, catching the seam allowances underneath. Stitch both sides in the same direction—working from the bottom of the item toward the top.

multiple rows of topstitching: Work with a twin or triple needle for perfectly parallel topstitching rows. The stitches will have some give, so this method is useful for sewing stretchy woven fabrics.

basting methods

Basting is a reliable way to hold fabric layers or fabric and trim together temporarily. Basting is especially helpful when working with slippery fabrics, matching prints or plaids, and applying trims. Baste with thread of a contrasting color to make it easier to see the stitches when it's time to remove them.

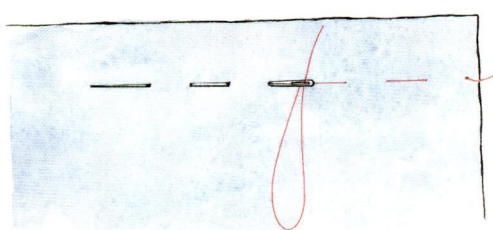

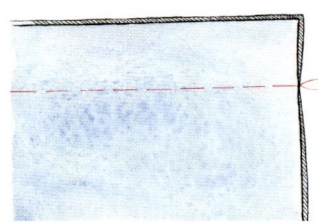

hand basting: This technique requires a long running stitch. Insert the needle in and out of the surface of the fabric to make several evenly spaced, ½" (1.3 cm) stitches. Pull the needle and thread through and repeat.

machine basting: This technique is effective when gathering. Adjust the machine-stitch length to the longest straight stitch, 3 to 6 stitches per inch (2.5 cm).

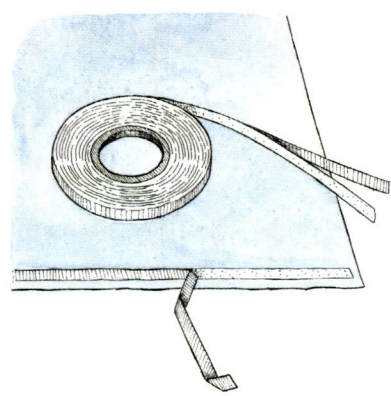

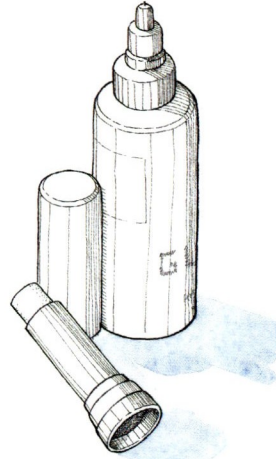

basting tape: This very narrow tape has adhesive on both sides, with a removable paper backing. Simply position the tape and press it in place with your fingers. Avoid stitching through it, as it will gum up your needle.

fabric glue: A glue stick or water-soluble glue, packaged in a tube applicator, temporarily holds fabric layers together to make it easier to sew the permanent stitches precisely.

types of seams

For most home décor sewing, you sew a plain seam, with ½" (1.3 cm) seam allowances and a stitch length of 8 to 12 stitches per inch (2.5 cm). For heavy fabrics, you may need a seam that has fewer stitches per inch (2.5 cm). For lightweight fabrics, you may need more stitches per inch (2.5 cm). If the seam puckers as you sew, shorten the stitch length.

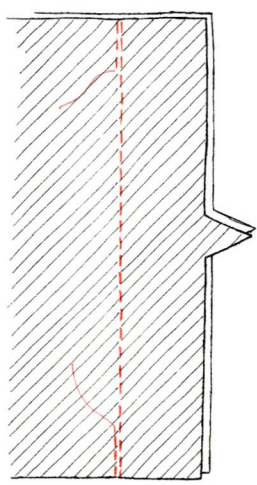

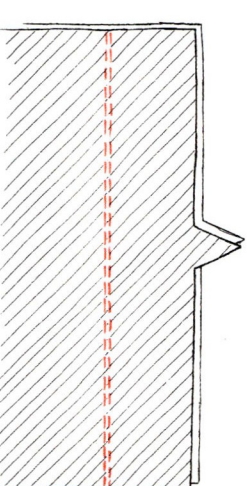

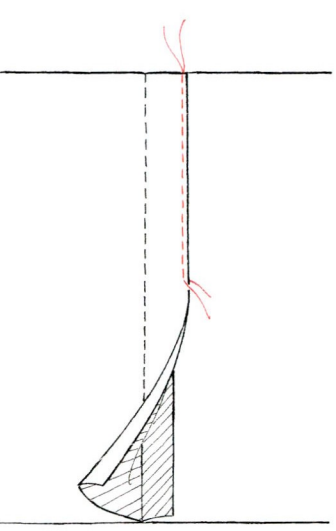

plain seam: This is the type of seam you'll use most often. With right sides together, stitch ½" (1.3 cm) from the edge. Backstitch two to three stitches at the beginning and end of the seam. Press the seam flat and then press open.

reinforced plain seam: This seam is especially effective on heavy, loosely woven fabrics. Sew a plain seam and then sew another line of stitching ⅛" (3 mm) away, inside the seam allowance. Press both seam allowances together to one side.

flat-fell seam: This style of seam adds strength to the construction. With wrong sides together, sew a wide, ¾" (1.9 cm) seam. Press the seam allowances to one side. Trim the lower seam allowance by half. Press under ¼" (6 mm) of the upper seam allowance, and pin it down, concealing the trimmed edge. Edgestitch along the fold.

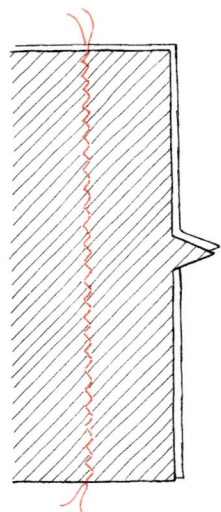

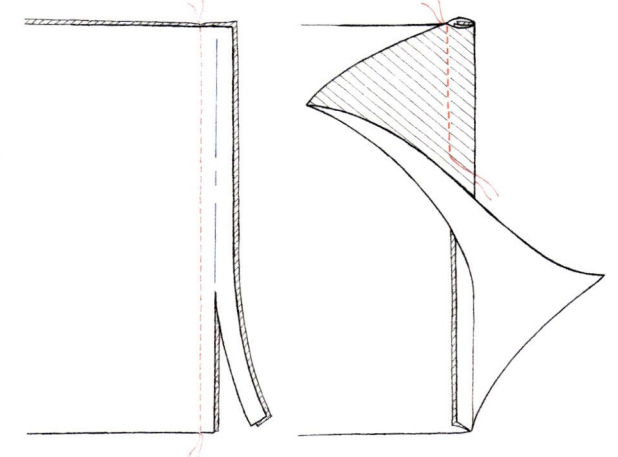

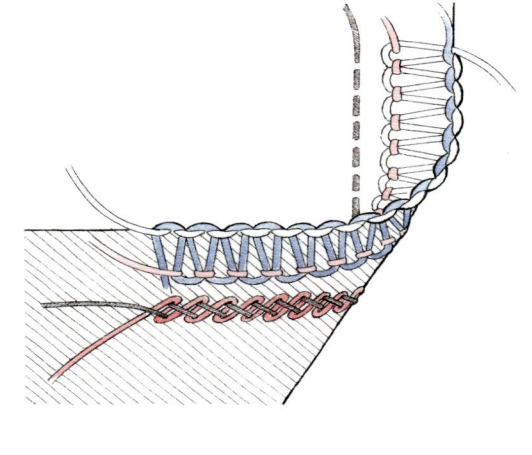

narrow zigzag: This stitch prevents puckers by building stretch into the seam. It is effective with loose weaves and stretch fabrics. Set the machine for a narrow zigzag stitch and sew as you would a plain seam.

french seam: This type of seam is best for lightweight, sheer fabrics and visible seams. With wrong sides together, sew a ¼" (6 mm) seam. Trim the allowances to ⅛" (3 mm) and press to one side.

Fold the right sides together (enclosing the trimmed seam), with the stitching line on the fold. Stitch ¼" (6 mm) from the folded edge. Press the seam to one side.

4-thread or 5-thread overlock stitch: This stitch is suited to most types of seams, especially exposed seams. Stitch the seam with a serger (overlock machine), trimming the seam allowances and overcasting both raw edges together at the same time.

trimming seams

Pressing is often enough to make seams lie flat—but sometimes you need to trim the seam allowances to reduce bulk. Trimming also helps smooth curves and sharpen corners. Trim the corner, clip, or notch before finishing the seam allowance.

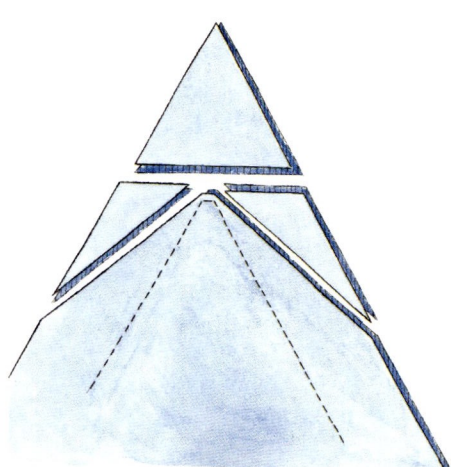

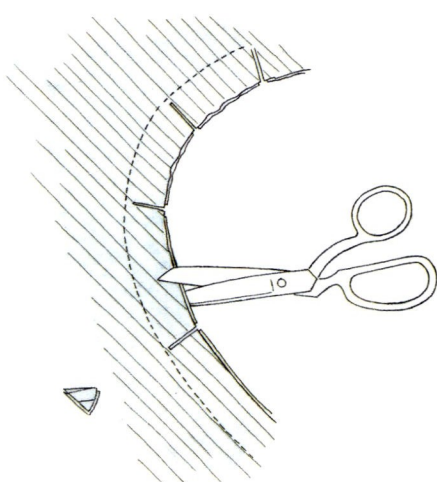

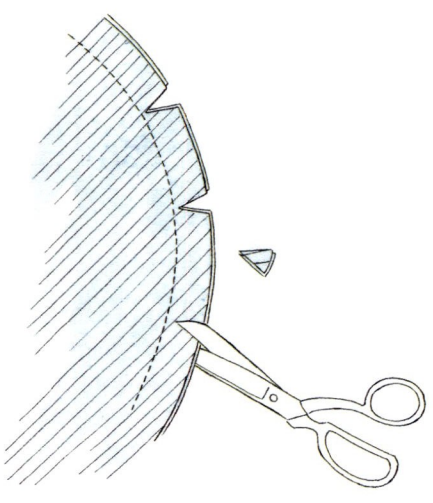

trimming a point or corner: First, trim the seam allowances straight across the point or corner. Then taper the allowances along each side.

clipping: Cut short snips into the seam allowance of inward curves—working with only the tips of the scissors—to help them lie flat. Cut up to, but not through, the stitching.

notching: Cut small wedges out of the seam allowances of outward curves to remove extra fullness.

seam finishes

For a neat and professional finish, you should finish all your seams (unless the project has a lining, which will conceal them). Finished seams also add durability to items you will launder regularly. Flat-fell and French seams (pages 82-83) already enclose the fabric's raw edges, so they don't require further finishing.

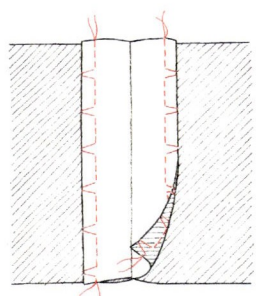

machine overedge: Press open the seam and set your machine to a built-in stitch that combines straight and zigzag stitches. Stitch along the edges of the seam allowances.

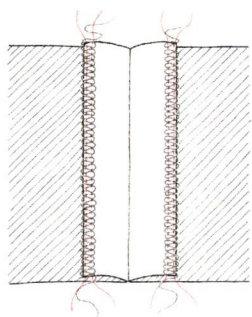

overlock: Any two-, three-, or four-thread overlock stitch, made with a serger or overlock machine, produces a professional-looking finish.

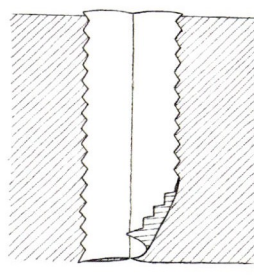

pinked edge: Working with pinking shears, cut a sawtooth edge along each seam allowance. A pinked edge is the simplest type of seam finish, although it does not entirely eliminate raveling.

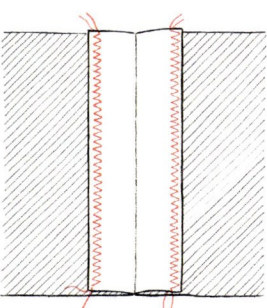

zigzag: Press the seam open. Set the machine to stitch a wide, medium-length zigzag. Stitch along the edge of each seam allowance so the stitches enclose the raw edge to prevent raveling. For lightweight fabrics, zigzag the seam allowances together along their edges and press to one side.

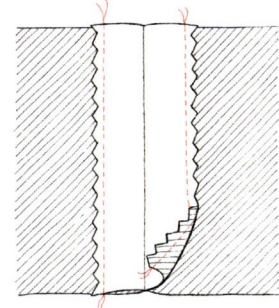

stitch and pink: Press the seam open and stitch 1/4" (6 mm) from the edge of each seam allowance. Cut the edge with pinking shears. This finish is more effective than pinking alone.

piecing fabric widths

Many home décor items require large expanses of fabric. Although most decorator fabric is available in wide widths—up to 120" (3 m)—you may sometimes need to piece fabric to create a panel that is wide enough for your project.

A center seam detracts from the appearance of any type of item. When piecing, arrange the fabric so there is one full-width center panel and two partial-width side panels.

To make the panels, work with two full widths of fabric. Cut one of the full-width fabrics in half. Stitch one half to each side of the other fabric, with $1/2$" (1.3 cm) seam allowances. Zigzag or overlock the seam allowances together, and press them away from the center panel. Very large projects—like curtains and draperies—may need several whole widths and/or half-widths of fabric.

If the fabric is striped or plaid or has a large printed pattern or motif, you will need extra fabric so that you can match the design at the joining seams (page 92). Include an extra pattern repeat in your yardage calculations for each width of fabric you'll need.

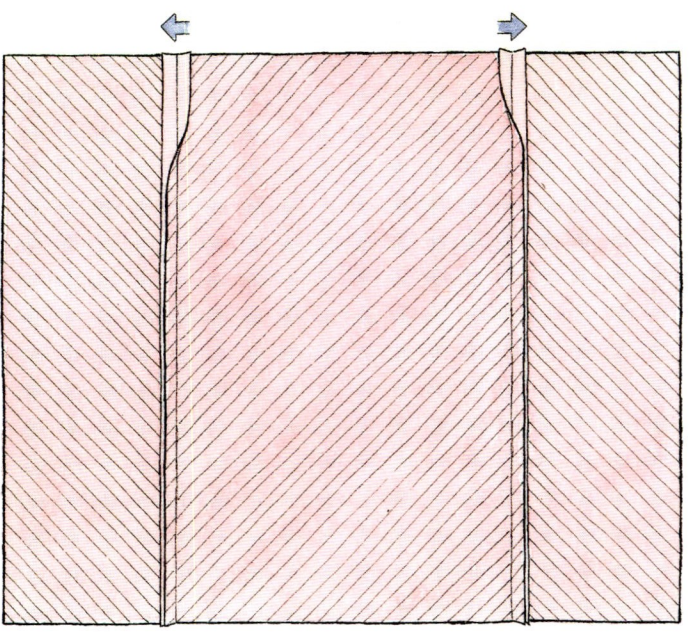

Before piecing fabric pieces, trim away the selvages — they will cause the stitched seam to pucker.

sewing textured fabrics

Rich surface textures add extra interest and dimension to your home décor. You can choose fabrics with multicolor or single-color designs woven right into the structure or fabrics with a three-dimensional, looped, brushed, or plush surface. Each requires special layout and sewing considerations.

When working with fabric that has an overall design, you usually need to buy extra fabric. Match the pattern at seams if you are making large projects—like window treatments and bed covers (page 92). Center the focal point of a design on pillows and cushions.

Fabrics with surface texture have nap—the fibers on the surface have a natural up and down direction. Lay out and cut all the pieces for your project in the same direction to avoid uneven shading.

Types of Textured Fabrics

Embellished Fabrics	Pile & Napped Fabrics
Brocade	Corduroy
Matelassé	Fleece
Dotted Swiss	Brushed Cotton
Moiré	Velvet/Velveteen
Tapestry	Chenille
Quilted fabric	Faux Fur
Lace	Suede or Ultrasuede

Rub your hand across the fabric. If the fabric feels rough, you are rubbing against the nap; notice the surface color in this direction is deeper. If the fabric feels smooth, you are rubbing with the nap; the surface is smoother, lighter, and shinier. You can cut your pieces with the nap running in either direction—just be consistent.

Sew a standard, straight seam for most textured and napped fabrics. If the fabric is heavy, use longer stitches, about 5 to 8 stitches per inch (2.5 cm) and hold the fabric taut. Stitch in the same direction as the nap.

Avoid seam finishes that add bulk. To reduce bulk on heavy pile fabrics, trim away the extra fibers from the seam allowance. For fabrics that ravel, pink the edges or finish them with an overedge stitch. Press pile fabrics face down on a needle board, terrycloth towel, or a piece of the same fabric, so you don't crush them.

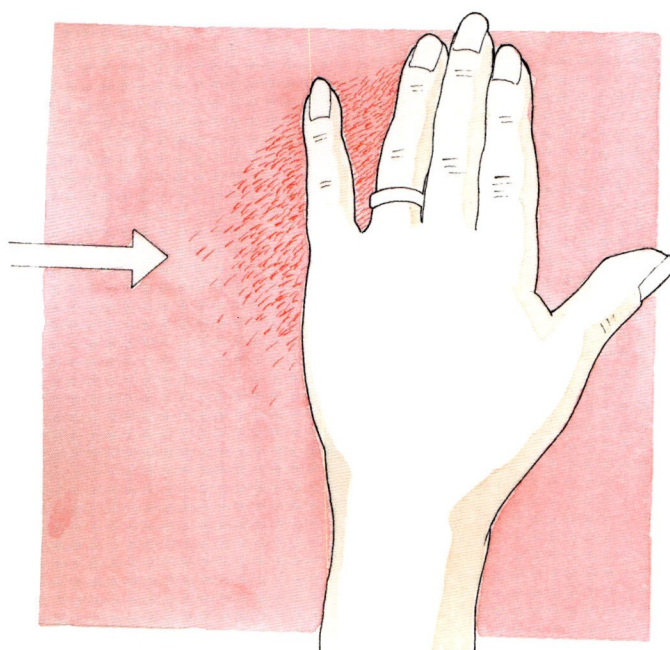

sewing sheer fabrics

Sheer decorator fabrics, usually made of polyester, are strong and stable. They are well suited for window treatments, like curtains and scarf swags. Construction details should be neat and seams should be clean-finished because they're visible on the right side of the fabric (page 85).

Most sheers are machine-washable, so prewash them before cutting. Even if the fabric doesn't shrink, prewashing removes resins that can cause skipped stitches. Sheer fabrics tend to fray, so zigzag-stitch or serge the cut edges before you wash them.

Types of Sheer Fabrics

Crisp Sheers	Soft Sheers
Dimity	Crepe Chiffon
Organdy	Batiste
Organza	Chiffon
Dotted Swiss	Georgette
Handkerchief Linen	
Voile	

Sew crisp sheers as you would sew other fabrics. Soft, flimsy sheers tend to slide and creep, so it easier to sew them with a straight-stitch presser foot and single-hole throat plate, if you have them. Set the machine to a short stitch length and sew slowly. A roller or even-feed presser foot (page 9) will also minimize slippage.

essential techniques

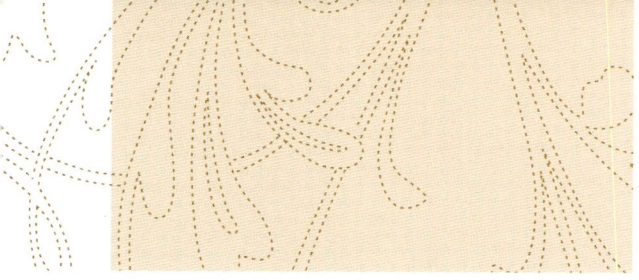

If the seams pucker on a soft sheer, place tissue paper over and under the fabric, and stitch through all four layers—or position tear-away stabilizer under the fabric. Carefully remove the paper after stitching the seam.

If the soft sheer bunches or is pulled into the machine at the beginning of the seam, place a small square of tear-away stabilizer under the fabric for the first few stitches. Stitch through all the layers and then continue stitching on the sheer fabric. Carefully remove the stabilizer after finishing the seam.

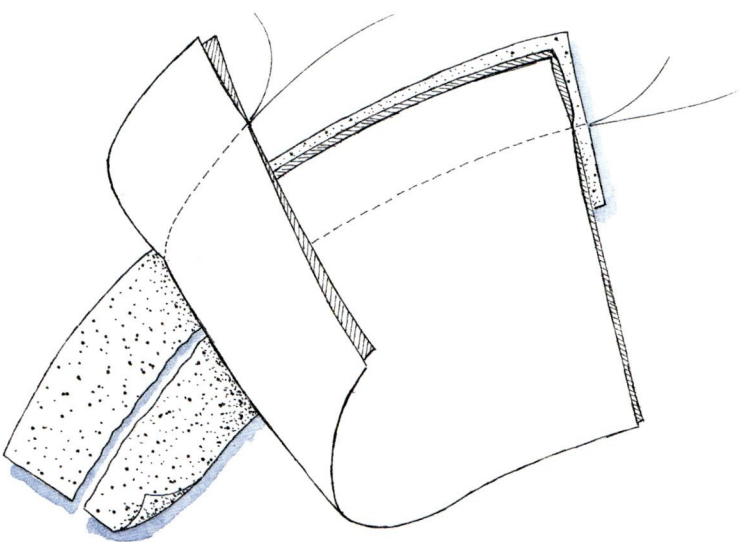

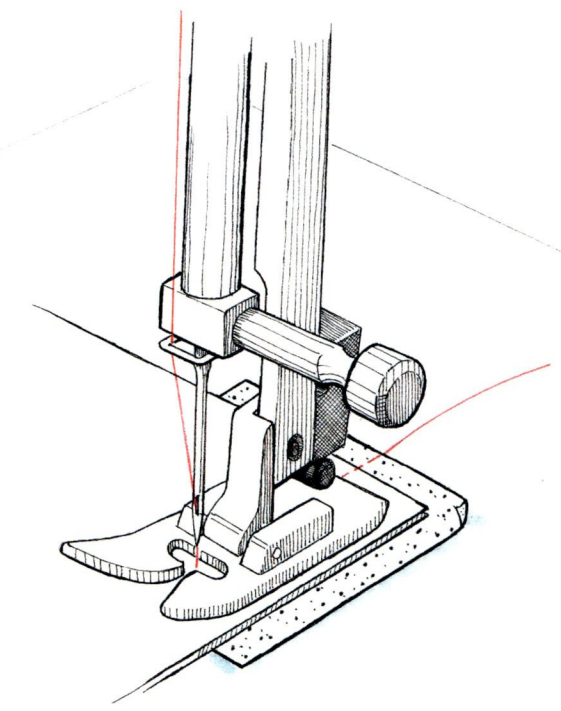

sewing stripes, plaids & prints

You'll need extra fabric if you are making large items—such as window treatments or bedding—with plaid, stripe, or print fabrics. The design repeats at regular intervals across the surface of the fabric, so you'll need to carefully join fabric widths so you don't interrupt the pattern.

The distance between one motif and the same point on the next identical motif is called a *pattern repeat*. The repeat is often marked on the selvage of the fabric. Add the length of the repeat to your yardage for each piece you need to cut.

Layout Guidelines

Stripes	Plaids	Checks	Small Overall Prints	Medium Overall Prints	Large Prints	Geometric Prints
• center or balance dominant stripe in small items • match horizontal stripes • continue stripe sequence, uninterrupted, across seams	• center or balance dominant bars in small items • match pattern both vertically and horizontally • cut woven plaids by following a bar in the plaid • make sure printed plaids are on the grain (page 21)	• match pattern both vertically and horizontally • cut woven checks by following one bar in the check • make sure printed checks are on the grain (page 21)	• don't need to match at seams • may be directional	• match at seams for large items • balance design for small items	• match at seams for large items • center dominant motif in small items (pillows, cushions) • may need extra fabric for multiple, identical small items	• match at seams, as for plaids and checks • balance placement of design for small items

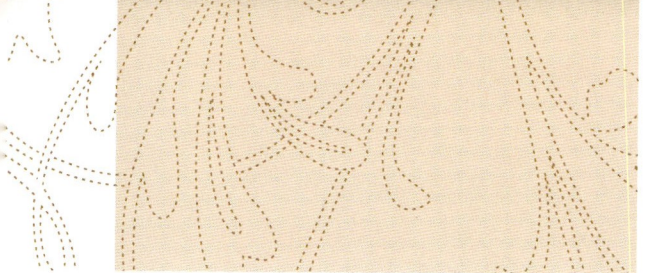

Matching Stripes, Plaids and Prints

1 Place two fabric widths right sides together, aligning the selvages. Fold back the upper selvage 1" (2.5 cm) and shift the pieces slightly up or down until the pattern matches exactly. Press the fold line.

2 Keeping the layers in place, unfold the pressed selvage and pin the fabric widths together, inserting the pins in the fold line. Turn the fabric over and check the match from the right side.

3 Stitch the seam, following the fold line and removing pins as you come to them. Check the match from the right side and make adjustments if necessary.

4 Trim away the selvages, leaving ½" (1.3 cm) seam allowances. Trim the upper and lower edges of the fabric panel evenly to the desired cut length.

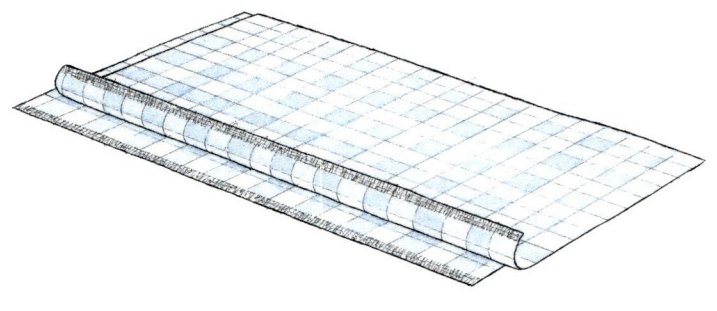

1

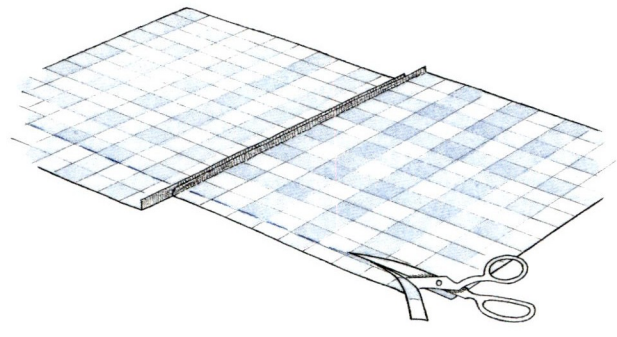

4

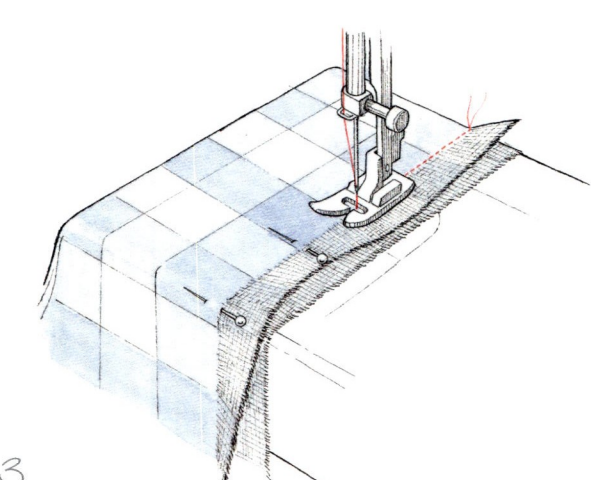

3

Roll out your length of fabric and stand back to find the dominant design motif, stripe, or bar. Sometimes you may see an unexpected secondary pattern.

stitching & mitering corners

The key to a perfectly shaped corner is the seam allowance. Reduce bulk by stitching and trimming the allowance or by mitering. Mitering—which is great for hemming—joins two adjacent edges diagonally with a neat, flat finish.

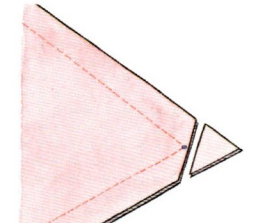

Stitching

Stitch the seam, stopping two or three stitches from the corner. Turn the hand wheel toward you to make the last few stitches. To turn the corner, keep the needle in the fabric, raise the presser foot, and pivot the fabric. Lower the presser foot and continue stitching. Trim the fabric, cutting diagonally to remove the corner point.

Mitering

1. Press all seam allowances to the wrong side to crease the fabric. Open the allowances. Fold the corner diagonally so the crease marks line up at the seam lines, as shown in the drawing. Press the fold to create a stitching guide.

2. Open the fabric and refold, right sides together, bringing together the crease marks in the corner seam allowance. Stitch along the pressed diagonal fold.

3. Trim the corner seam allowance to $\frac{3}{8}$" (1 cm) and press open.

4. Turn the seam allowances to the wrong side and press, forming a flat, mitered corner.

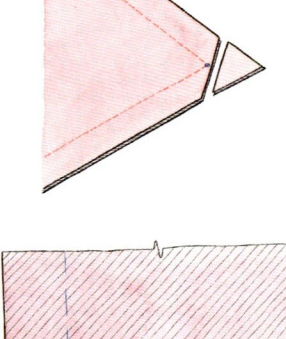

1

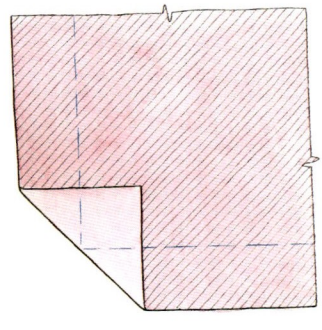

3

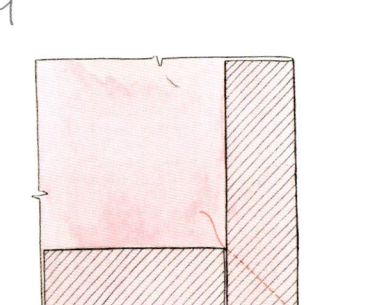

2

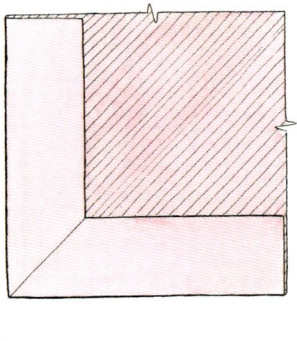

4

attaching trims

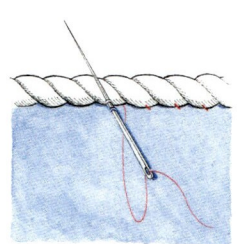

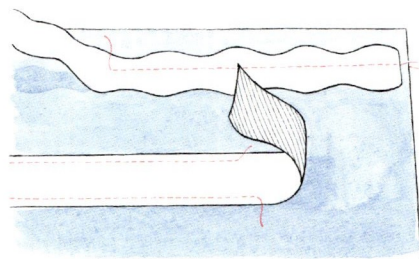

There are several ways to apply decorative trims, depending on the kind of trim you choose and the way in which you want to use it.

Before you begin, mark placement lines for the trim with a water- or air-soluble pen. If pins will damage the trim or fabric, use a glue stick or fabric adhesive to temporarily hold the trim in place while you sew.

hand stitching: Attach bulky trims by hand. Slipstitch (page 78) the trim to the fabric, with thread that is the same color as the fabrics.

machine stitching: Hold the trim in place with basting tape or fabric adhesive. Machine-stitch down the center of narrow trims or along both long edges of wide trims.

mitering trim: Pin the trim along the placement line until it reaches the corner. Topstitch both edges, stopping at the line. Fold the trim back on itself and finger-press. Fold the trim diagonally to form a right angle and align the edges with the placement lines.

Refold the trim back on itself and stitch directly through the diagonal crease. Fold the trim back down so it turns the corner neatly. Topstitch along both edges.

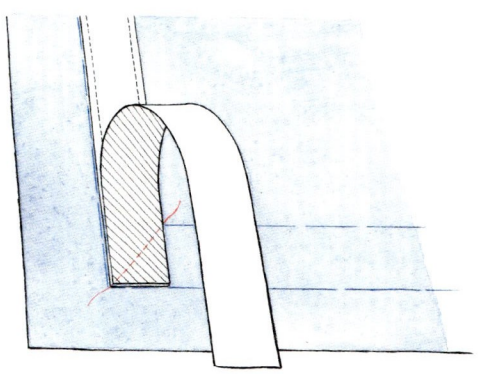

Do not pull trim taut when sewing. Stitch slowly, easing the trim around corners so it will lie flat. Try not to cut the trim until you reach the end of each section.

bias tape or binding: Open the bias tape and, with right sides together, pin it to the fabric, matching the edges. Stitch in the fold line of the tape, close to the raw edge.

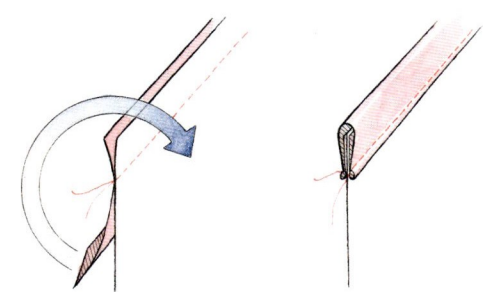

Refold the bias tape and wrap it over the raw edge. On the right side of the fabric, edgestitch the tape in place (page 79), catching the underlayer.

fold-over braid: Encase the raw fabric edge with the braid, placing the narrower edge on the right side of the fabric. Baste through all layers. Topstitch on the right side of the fabric (page 80), close to the edge.

edging in a seam: Place the unfinished edge of the trim along the fabric edge, right sides together and baste. Pin the two fabric layers together with the edging in between. Stitch.

applied edging: If the heading is decorative, sew it directly to the right side of the fabric. If not, lap the folded or hemmed fabric edge over the heading and topstitch. Or sew the trim on the right side of the fabric and cover it with ribbon.

welting: Follow the same process as when edging in a seam. Work with a zipper foot so you can stitch as close as possible to the trim (page 99).

tassels: Hand-sew tassels in place with heavy thread.

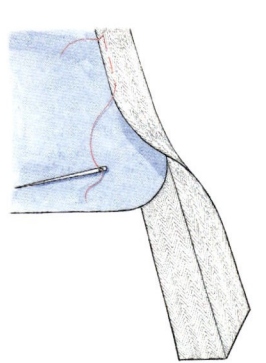
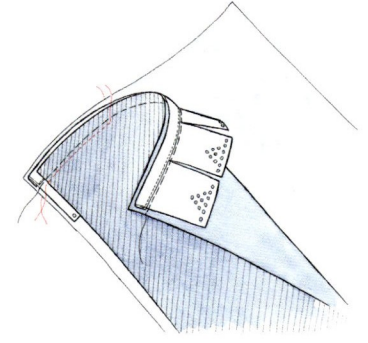
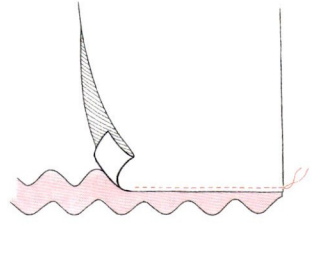
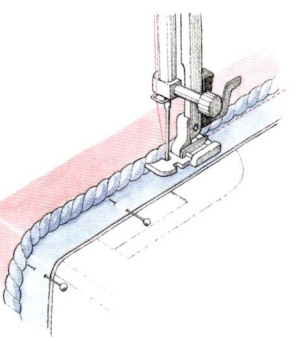

If the home décor item will be dry-cleaned, attach trim simply by gluing it in place with fabric glue.

making bias binding

Bias tape, or binding encloses fabric edges for a neat, often decorative, finish. Because of the bias grain direction, the binding wraps around curves without puckering. You can purchase binding in an assortment of colors. Or, for a perfect match, you can easily make your own single-fold or double-fold binding.

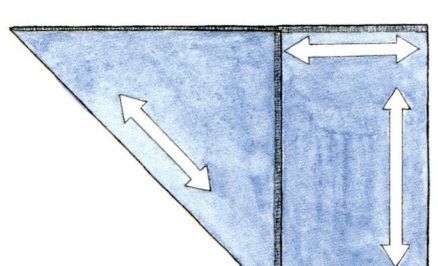

1. Fold the fabric diagonally so that one selvage is at a right angle to the other selvage. Press along the fold—the direction of the fabric grain at the fold is the bias grain. Cut along the pressed line. Set aside the triangle of fabric.

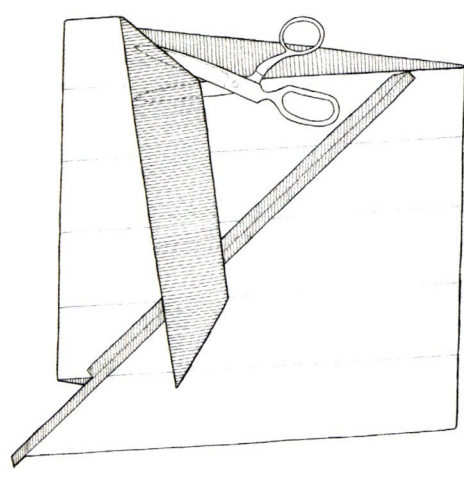

2. Multiply the desired finished width of the binding by four to determine how wide to cut the strips. For example, for a 1/4" (6 mm) finished binding, you'll need strips 1" (2.5 cm) wide.

Beginning at the diagonal cut edge of the fabric, measure and mark parallel lines that are the desired cut width. After you have drawn the last strip, discard the triangular remnant—or save it as scrap.

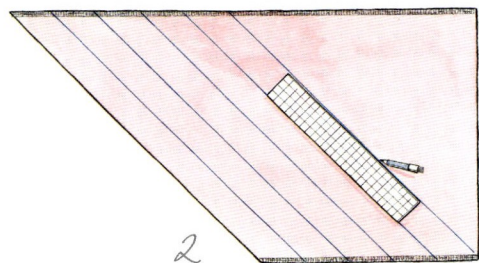

3. Fold the fabric right sides together, matching selvages to form an irregular tube. Match the marked lines so that one strip of fabric extends beyond the tube on each side. Sew a 1/4" (6 mm) seam and press it open. Starting at one end, work around the tube to cut a continuous strip along the marked line.

4. Press both long edges to the center of the tape, taking care not to distort the width of the strip. Press the strip in half again to create a double-fold bias tape.

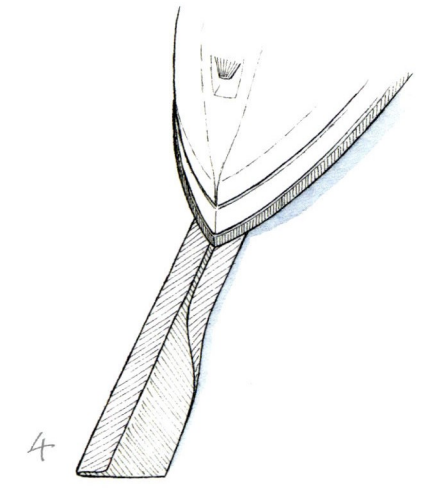

mitering bias trim

Bias trim provides a sturdy, decorative edge finish on placemats, tablecloths, curtains, and draperies. A mitered corner adds a smooth, neat finish.

1 Press open the bias tape. Beginning in the center of one side, stitch the right side of the bias tape to the wrong side of the fabric, aligning the edges. Slow the machine and pivot precisely at the corner. Continue stitching, pivoting at all corners.

2 Trim the seam allowance diagonally at each corner. Fold the bias tape so it forms a right angle and the fold aligns with the stitching. Finger-press the fold.

3 Unfold the bias tape so it extends over the seam. Stitch on the finger-pressed fold. Trim off the point at the corner.

4 Finger-press to open the mitered seam. Turn the bias tape to the right side and press. Topstitch the edge of the tape to encase the edge of the fabric.

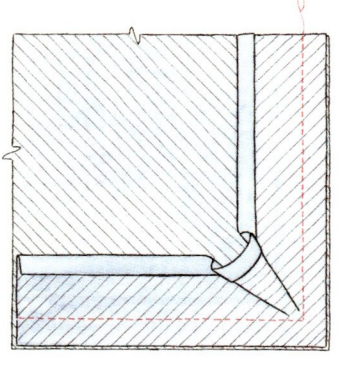

1

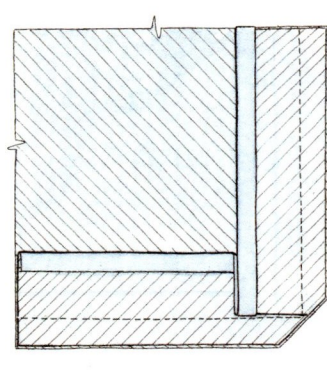

2

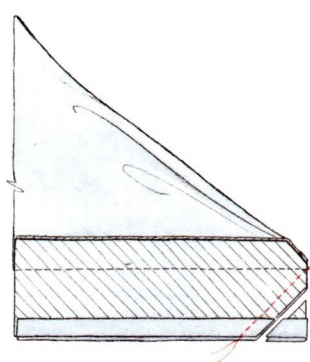

3

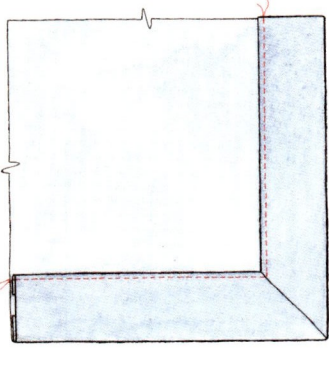

4

making welting

Welting creates a well-defined edge finish on many types of home décor items. You make welting by wrapping a strip of bias fabric around a filler cord. The cord can be either cotton or polyester and of various thicknesses.

The most common size welting for home décor sewing is $5/32"$ (0.16 cm) in diameter. Cut a bias strip that is $1^1/2"$ (3.8 cm) wide to cover a cord of that diameter. This size welting is appropriate for pillows, cushions, slipcovers, table runners, and placemats.

For welting thicker than $1/4"$ (6 mm) in diameter, wrap a piece of paper around the cord. Pin it close to the cord and trim the paper $1/2"$ (1.3 cm) from the pin. Measure the paper to determine the cut width of the bias strip. Attach thicker welting to large pillows, pillow shams, duvet covers and coverlets—or to any other item for a bold effect.

1 Cut bias strips as you would for bias binding (page 96, steps 1 through 3). Allow extra length so you can overlap the ends and ease the welting around corners as you sew.

2 Attach the zipper foot or piping foot to your machine (page 9). Wrap the bias strip, right side out, around the cord, keeping the raw edges even. Stitch right next to the cord, gently stretching the fabric as you sew.

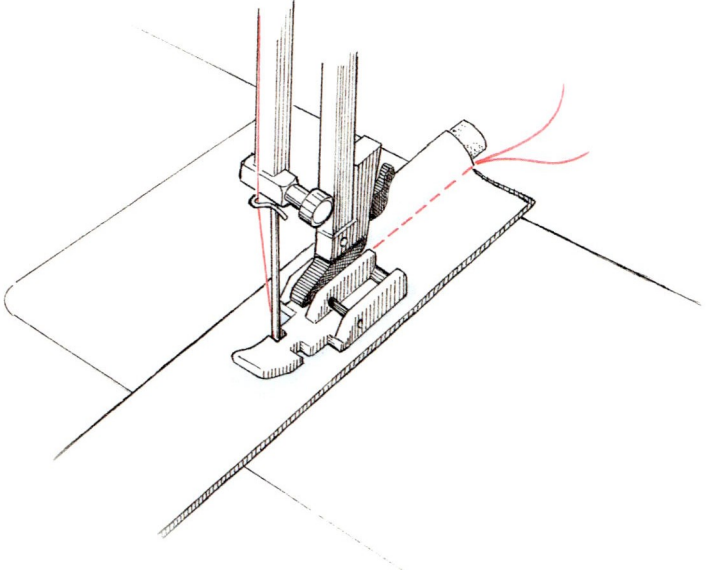

To avoid ripples in welting:
- pin or glue-baste the strip around the cord before stitching
- feed both layers of fabric evenly through the presser foot
- make sure the cord is not twisted within the fabric.

attaching welting

Welting reinforces the seams on a pillows, cushions, slipcovers, tiebacks, tablecloths, and bedcovers while adding a decorative, finishing touch.

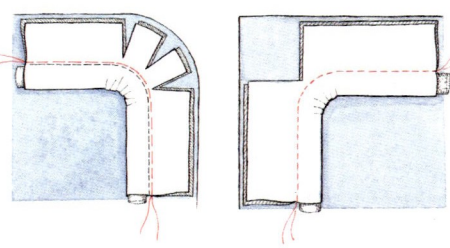

To ease welting around a curve, clip into the seam allowance up to the stitching several times. For sharp corners, cut once and trim away the seam allowance.

1   Place the welting on the right side of the fabric, aligning the edges of the seam allowances. Position it so the stitching will begin and end in the middle of one side of the pillow (not near a corner).

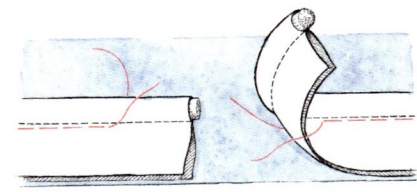

2   Machine-baste the welting just to the right of the seam line, leaving the first 2" (5.1 cm) and the last 2" (5.1 cm) of the welting free. Cut off the extra length, leaving a 1" (2. 5 cm) overlap.

3   With a seam ripper, remove 1" (2. 5 cm) of stitching on both ends of the welting. Pull back the fabric on one end and cut the cording so the ends abut.

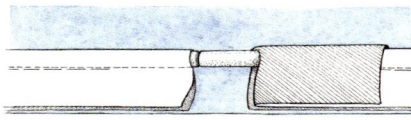

4   Fold under $1/2$" (1.3 cm) of fabric on that same end. Then wrap the fabric around the other end of the cording for a smooth joining. Finish stitching the welting.

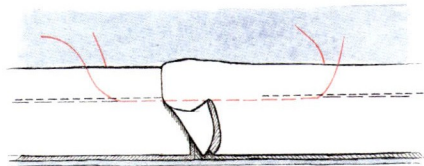

5   With the right sides together and the welting sandwiched between, sew together the two fabric pieces with a regular stitch length. Stitch directly over the basting stitches.

making fabric bows

Fabric bows are quick accents for window treatments, bedding, and pillows. Make a bow that ties and unties or a fixed bow with a permanent shape.

To determine the best size bow for your project—and how much fabric you'll need—tie a bow with fabric scrap, old ribbon, or a tape measure. Pin the bow in place to see how it looks and adjust as needed.

Untie the bow, measure the length, and add 1" (2.5 cm) for finishing the ends. Double the measurement and add 1" (2.5 cm) for the seam allowance. Cut a strip of fabric to your dimensions.

Tie Bow

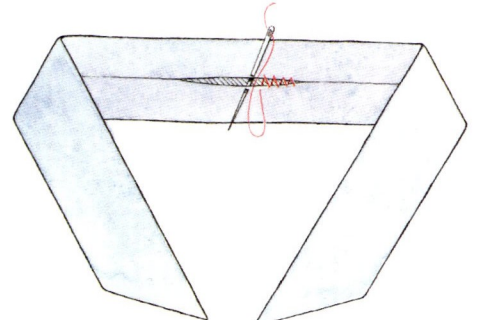

1   Fold the strip in half lengthwise, right sides together. Stitch ½" (1.3 cm) from the long cut edges, leaving a 3" (7.6 cm) opening near the center.

2   Center the seam and press it open, working only with the tip of the iron.

3   Stitch across the ends on a diagonal and trim. Turn the fabric right side out through the opening and press. Slipstitch the opening closed (page 78).

4   Tie the bow and hand-stitch it in position—or weave the ends through your project and tie the bow in place.

Fixed Bow

1   Follow steps 1 to 3 above. Tie the bow.

2   Cut a piece of fabric to make a knot cover. The fabric should be the same width as the bow fabric and 1" (2.5 cm) longer than the circumference of the knot.

3   Fold the fabric in half lengthwise, right sides together. Stitch ½" (1.3 cm) from the long edges. Turn the knot cover right side out, center the seam in the back, and press the ends to the inside.

Wrap the knot around the center of the bow and slipstitch the ends together in back (page 78). Stitch or glue the bow in place.

If your fabric needs more body, apply soft fusible interfacing (page 15) to the wrong side for a crisper bow.

making tassels

Tassels add elegance, whether stitched to the corners of a pillow, attached to a shade pull, or draped over a valance or swag. If you can't find the perfect tassels for your project, make your own with decorative cords, threads, and yarns.

1 Cut a piece of heavy cardboard the desired length of the tassel and about 3" (7.6 cm) wide. Wrap the yarns around the length of the cardboard until the bundle looks full (at least 100 times).

2 Thread a tapestry needle with a double strand of yarn. Slide the needle under the yarns at the top of the cardboard, remove the needle, and tie the bundle securely. Cut straight across the yarns at the opposite end and remove the cardboard.

3 Wrap a double length of yarn several times around the tassel, about 1¼" (3 cm) from the top, and tie it securely. Thread the tail onto the tapestry needle and bring the needle out at the top of the tassel. Work with the yarn tail to slipstitch the tassel to the fabric (page 78). Or hand-sew two tassels to a length of cord—one at each end—to make a decorative tie.

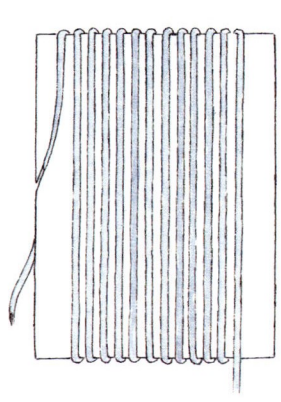

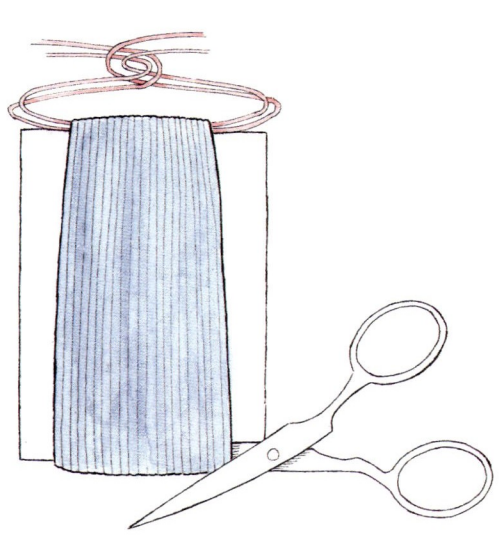

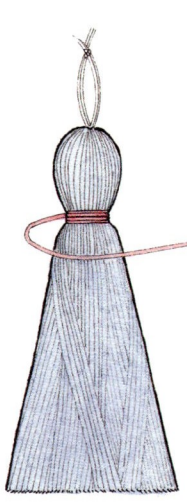

forming gathers

Gathers are a series of tiny, soft folds that create shape and interest. The folds distribute the fullness of the fabric evenly—along a ruffle or the top of a curtain, for example. Gathers are easy to make. Simply straight-stitch and adjust the fabric by hand.

1   Set your machine to its longest straight stitch (basting stitch). Loosen the upper thread tension slightly. Thread the bobbin with a contrasting color of thread for greater visibility.

2   On the right side of the fabric, stitch two parallel lines in the seam allowance—one just inside the stitching line and the other ¼" (6 mm) away. Leave long thread tails at both ends. If the fabric is long, break the basting stitches at the halfway mark and gather each half separately.

3   Pin the basted fabric to the corresponding fabric, right sides together. The piece with the basting stitches will be the longer piece. Secure the threads at one end by wrapping them around a straight pin to form a figure eight.

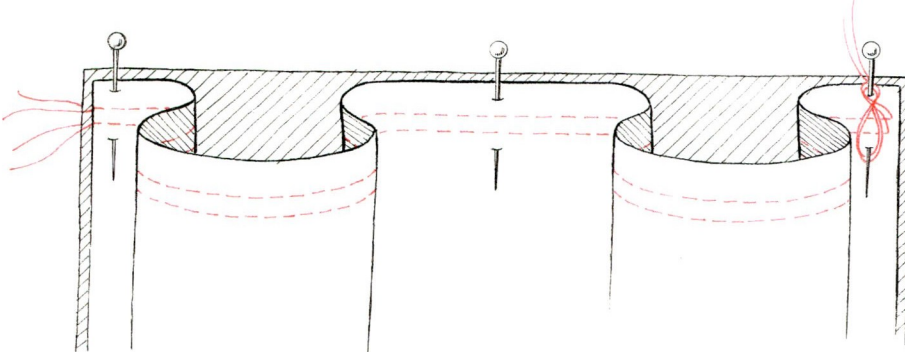

4   From the other end, gently pull the bobbin threads, sliding the fabric along the threads to distribute it evenly.

5   When the gathered piece "fits" the straight piece, pin the layers together at close intervals (about every 1" [2.5 cm]). As you pin, adjust the gathers with a pin or with your fingernail to distribute them evenly.

6   Change to a standard stitch length and normal upper-thread tension. With the gathered side up, machine-stitch a 1/2" (1.3 cm) seam. Remove pins as you sew and hold the fabric taut on both sides of the needle to keep the gathers from shifting or pleating.

7   Carefully press the seam allowances toward the flat, ungathered fabric with the tip of the iron. Do not press across the surface of the gathers or you will flatten them

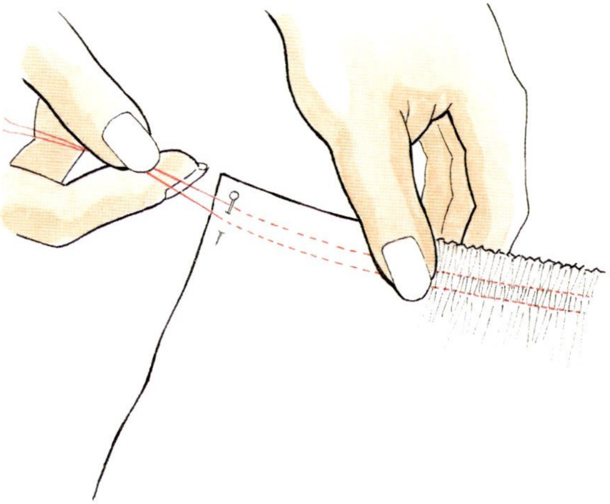

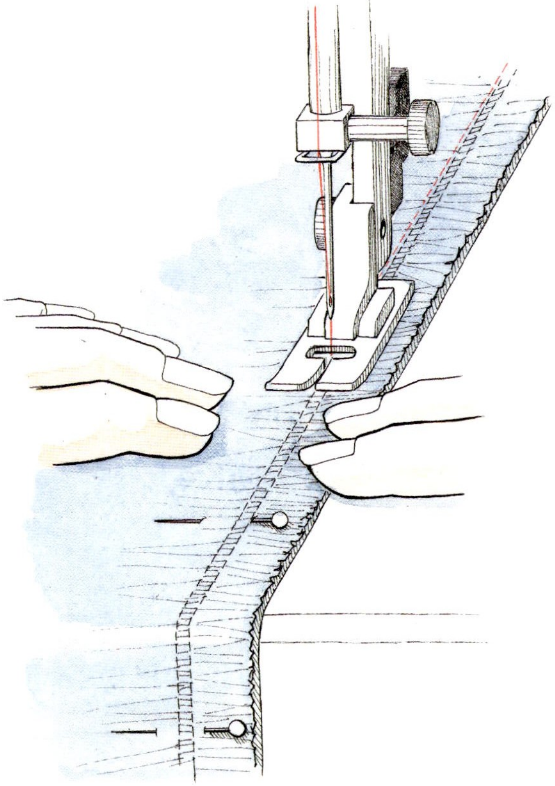

sewing ruffles

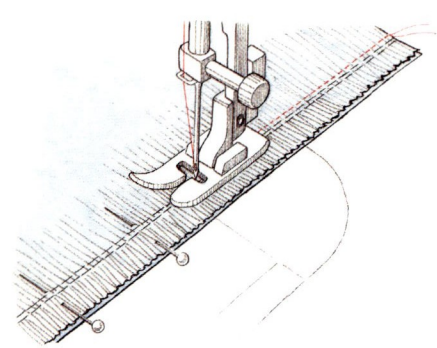

A ruffle is a strip of fabric that is gathered along one edge and attached to a flat piece of fabric—for example, a pillow, bed skirt, or tablecloth. The visible edge is finished. The gathered, raw edge is hidden in a seam or enclosed between two fabrics. Most ruffles are cut on the straight grain.

For a Hem Ruffle

1   Stitch the ruffle pieces together to form one long strip. Stitch a narrow hem on one long edge (page 48). Press.

2   Sew two rows of basting stitches along the opposite long edge, just inside the seam line. Pull the threads to form gathers (page 102).

3   Pin the ruffle, right sides together, to the fabric edge, aligning raw edges. Adjust the gathers so the fullness is distributed evenly. Stitch the ruffle in place. Remove the basting threads.

4   Trim the seam allowances. Zigzag-stitch or serge them together for a clean finish.

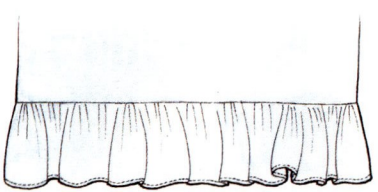

For an Enclosed Ruffle

1   Follow steps 1 through 3 for the hem ruffle.

2   Stitch the ruffle to the first fabric, distributing the fullness evenly. Pin the second piece to the first, right sides together, with the ruffle in between the pieces. Stitch with the first piece up so you can use the existing stitching line as a guide.

3   Turn the pieces right side out, so the ruffle extends from the outer edge.

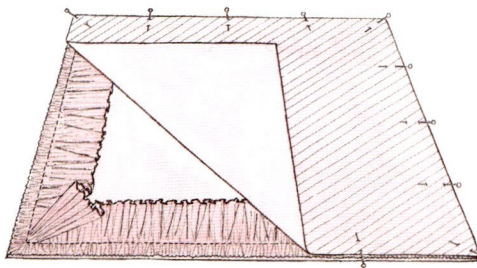

When applying a ruffle around corners, allow extra fullness at each corner so the ruffle lies flat.

sewing pleats

Pleats are fabric folds that are stitched in place. You can press them for a crisp, tailored look or let them hang in soft folds. They add dimension and visual interest to even the simplest valances and bed skirts.

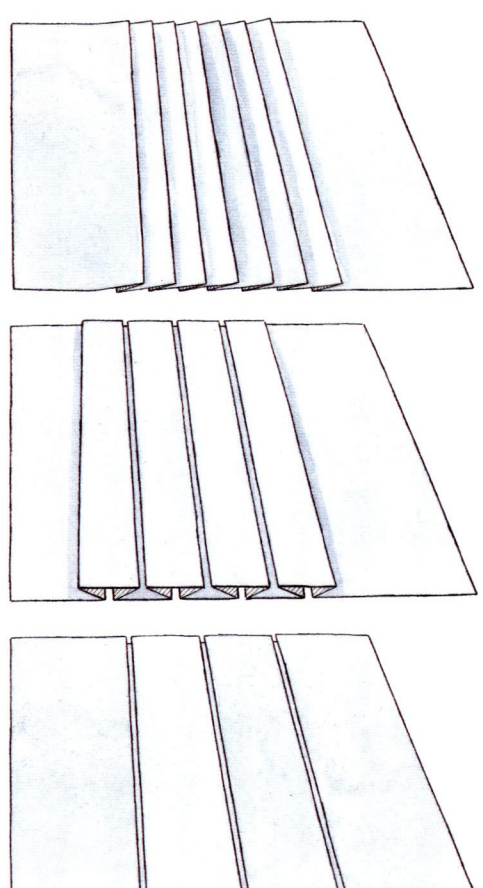

Make single pleats at corners, cluster them, or arrange them across a surface. You can also pleat large fabrics with heading tapes (page 75).

The best way to plan your pleats is to make a paper pattern. Cut a narrow piece of paper to the desired finish width. Add a $\frac{1}{2}$" (1.3 cm) seam allowance and the hardware return (if any) at each end. You need from 4" to 6" (10.2 to 15.2 cm) of fabric for each pleat, with $3\frac{1}{2}$" to 4" (8.9 to 10.2 cm) of fabric between each one.

Experiment to decide how many pleats you want, how wide they should be, and in which direction they will fold. Measure the width of the pleated pattern to determine yardage.

knife pleats: formed with a single fold line and placement line; folded pleats all face the same direction

box pleats: formed with two fold lines that fold to meet on the wrong side of the fabric; fabric pleats on the right side

inverted box pleats: same as box pleats, except folds meet on the right side of the fabric; pleat forms on the wrong side

Transfer the folds and placement lines from your paper pattern to the fabric with dressmaker's carbon paper and a tracing wheel.

Fold the fabric along each fold line to meet the placement line to form the pleat. Pin the entire length at regular intervals (knife pleats are shown in the drawing below). Baste across the seam allowance to hold the pleats in place. Stitch the pleated piece to the corresponding piece, as needed for the project.

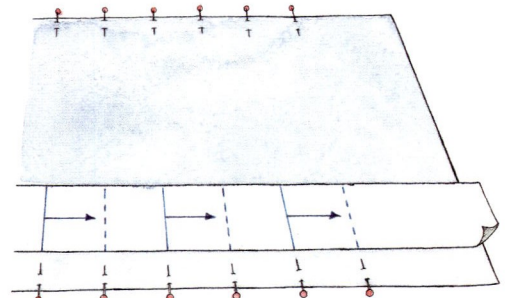

inserting a centered zipper

Centered zippers work well in knife-edge pillows (page 31) and boxed pillows (page 33). Cut slightly wider seam allowances—about ³⁄₄" (1.9 cm)—for any zipper opening.

1 Machine-baste the zipper opening closed. Clip the basting stitches every 2" (5.1 cm) so they are easy to remove later. Press the seam open. Finish the seam allowance edges with pinking or zigzag stitches (page 85).

2 Use a glue stick or basting tape to glue the zipper face-down on the wrong side of the decorator fabric. Center the teeth over the seam line and position the top stop 1" (2.5 cm) below the cut edge. Flip up the pull tab.

3 Place a pin below the bottom stop on the right side of the fabric. (Do not use tape on napped or delicate fabrics.) Center a piece of ¹⁄₂" (1.3 cm)-wide clear tape over the seam as a stitching guide. Remove the pin.

4 Attach the zipper foot and adjust so it is to the right of the needle. Begin stitching at the seam at the bottom of the tape. Stitch across the bottom of the zipper, pivot at the edge of the tape, and stitch up the side, using the edge of the tape as a guide.

5 Adjust the zipper foot to the left of the needle. Begin stitching at the seam at the bottom of the tape. Stitch up the side of the zipper.

6 Pull the thread tails to the wrong side and knot them at the bottom of the zipper. Remove the basting stitches and press with a press cloth (page 24).

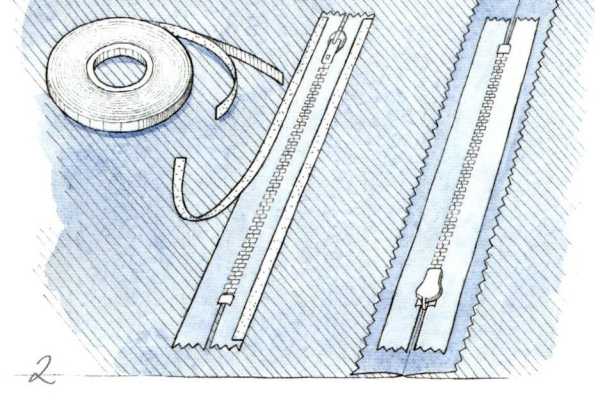

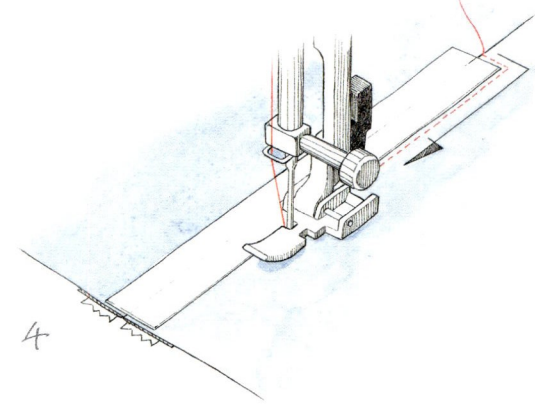

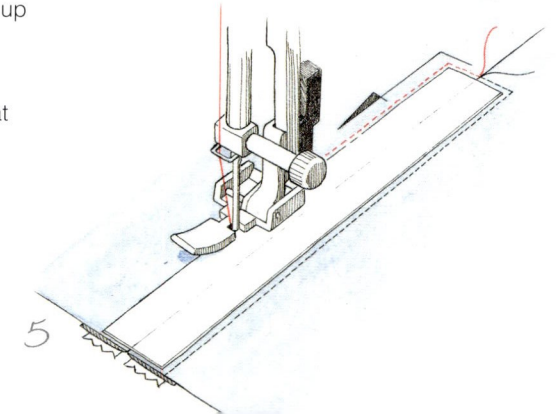

inserting a lapped zipper

Lapped zipper construction conceals the zipper a bit more than the center construction. This style of zipper works well when inserting zippers along an edge, as for a slipcover. Cut slightly wider seam allowances for the zipper opening.

1 Follow step 1 for the centered zipper construction. Open the zipper and place it facedown on the right-hand side of the seam allowance (with the open end facing you). Position the zipper coil directly over the seam line and position the top stop 1" (2.5 cm) below the cut edge. Flip up the tab. Pin, glue, or hand-baste the zipper tape to the seam allowance only.

2 Attach the zipper foot and adjust so it is to the right of the needle. Machine-baste from the bottom to the top of the zipper, as close to the edge of the coil as possible.

3 Close the zipper, turn the zipper faceup, and flip up the pull tab. Smooth the fabric away from the zipper, forming a narrow fold between the coil and the seam. Adjust the zipper foot to the left of the needle and, starting at the bottom of the zipper, stitch through the folded seam allowance and the zipper tape, as close as possible to the edge of the fold.

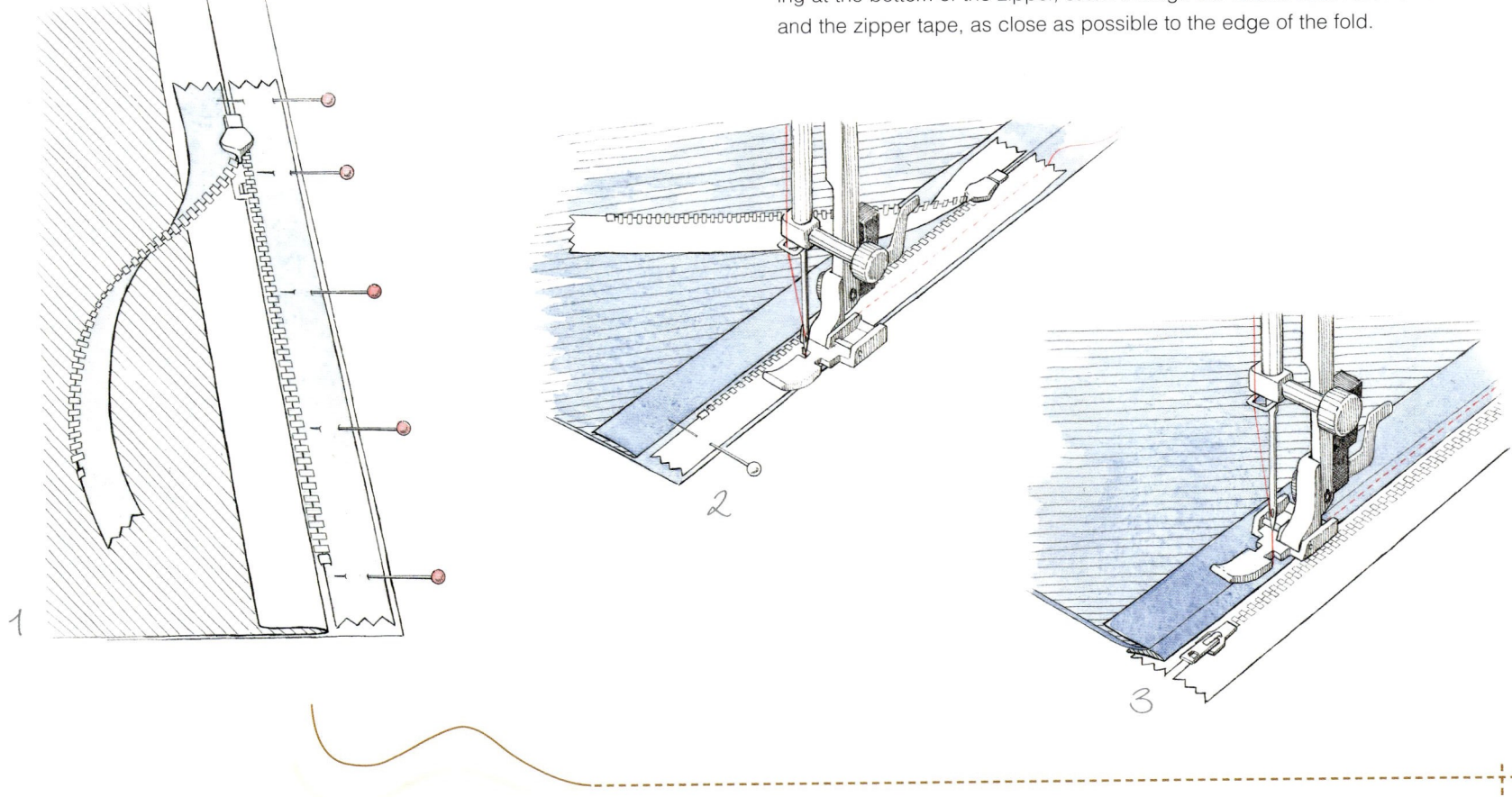

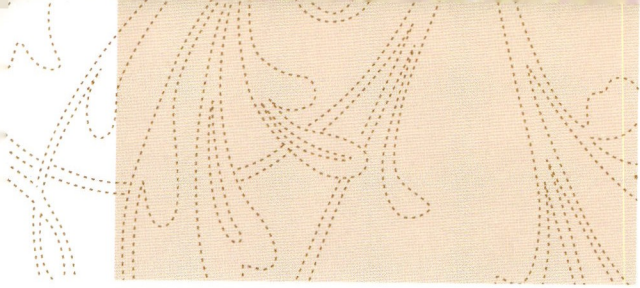

4 Turn the decorator fabric to the right side and spread the fabric as flat as possible. Mark the bottom of the zipper with a pin. Place ½" (1.3 cm)-wide clear tape along the right side of the seam to act as a topstitching guide. Starting at the seam at the bottom of the zipper, topstitch across the bottom and up the outside edge of the tape.

5 Remove the tape. Pull the thread tails to the wrong side and knot them. Remove the basting stitches and press. Press on a tailor's ham if the seam is curved.

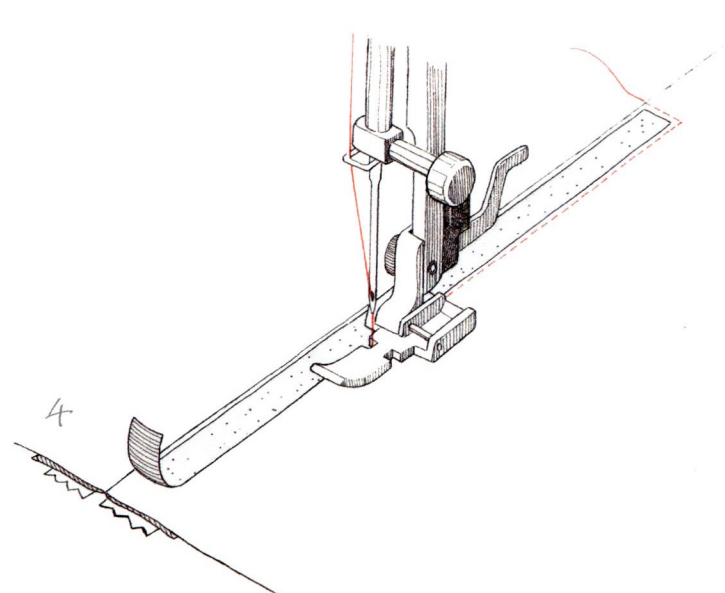

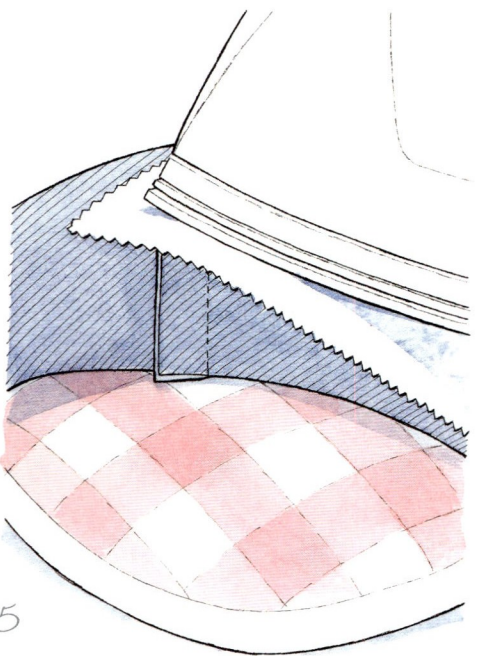

making buttonholes

Every sewing machine makes buttonholes differently. New and computerized machines make automatic, one-step buttonholes in several styles, but you can make quality buttonholes on any type of machine. Refer to your owner's manual for specific instructions

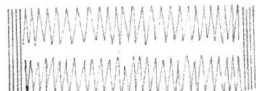

To make a standard bar-tack buttonhole, all you need is a simple zigzag stitch. Stabilize the fabric with a similar color of interfacing (page 14) to prevent the buttonhole from gaping or puckering. If the fabric is sheer or lightweight, use a tear-away stabilizer so you can remove it later (page 90).

To Determine Buttonhole Length

sew-through flat button: Measure the diameter and thickness of the button. Add ⅛" (3 mm) to those numbers.

shank button: Pin a thin strip of paper around the button. Slide the button out and measure between the pin marks. Add ⅛" (3 mm) to the measurement.

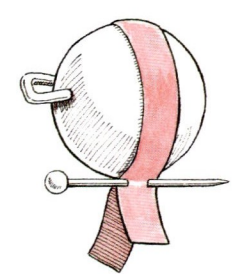

To Make a Buttonhole

1. Make a practice buttonhole on fabric scraps that have the exact same thickness as the layers of your project, including the interfacing.

2. Measure and mark evenly spaced buttonholes on the right side of the fabric.

3. To stitch the buttonholes, attach your buttonhole attachment and follow the instructions in your owner's manual.

4. Insert pins inside each end of the buttonhole so you don't cut through them. With small, sharp scissors or a seam ripper, carefully cut the fabric between the lines of stitching.

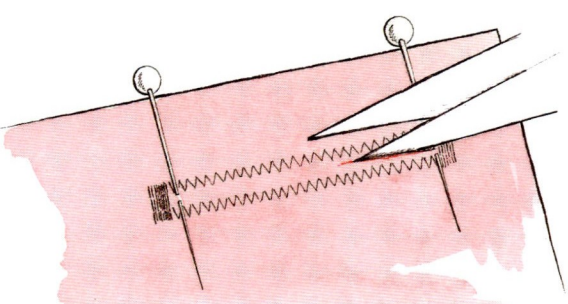

essential techniques

sewing on buttons

Buttons come in just about any type of material, but there are two basic styles: sew-through flat buttons and shank buttons. Sew-through buttons have two or four holes for stitching. Shank buttons have a stem with a single hole. Buttons can be functional (for example, as closures for pillow and duvet covers) or decorative (as accents on a tab-top window treatment).

Flat Button
(for lightweight fabrics and decorative styles)

1 Thread the needle and knot the ends.

2 Bring the needle through one hole and back down through the opposite hole and the fabric several times. If there are four holes, stitch through the other two holes the same way.

3 Knot the thread on the wrong side of the fabric.

Flat Button with Thread Shank
(for medium- to heavy-weight fabrics)

1 Thread the needle and knot the ends. Bring the needle up from the wrong side of the fabric and insert it through one buttonhole. Place a toothpick on top of the button. Bring the needle down through the opposite hole. Take about six stitches. If there are four holes, do the same for the other two holes.

2 Remove the toothpick and lift the button away from the fabric. Bring the needle out between the button and the fabric surface. Wind the thread around the stitches to create a thread shank. Take two or three tiny stitches on the wrong side of the fabric and knot the ends.

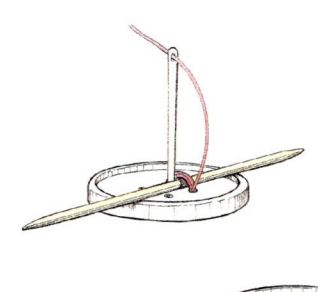

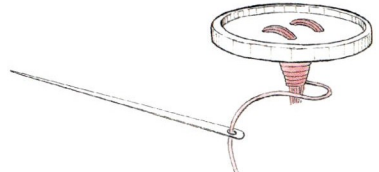

Shank Button
(for medium- to heavy-weight fabrics)

1 Thread the needle and knot the ends.

2 Position the button with the shank hole perpendicular to the fabric surface. Attach the button by sewing several stitches through the shank. Take two or three tiny stitches on the wrong side of the fabric and knot the ends.

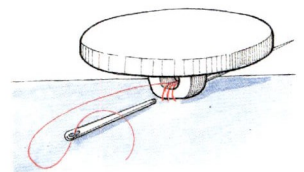

Make your own fabric-covered shank buttons. Store-bought kits include the button parts and complete instructions.

hemming methods

Home décor items are almost always hemmed by machine—and usually you'll make a double-fold hem. Hems may be located at the bottom, sides, or at the top.

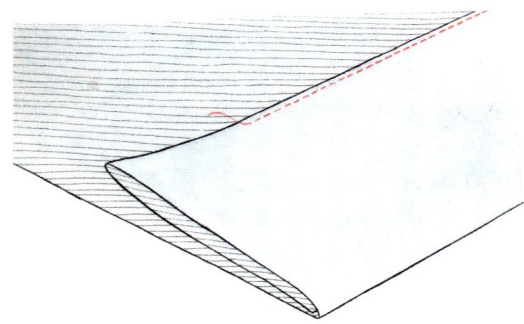

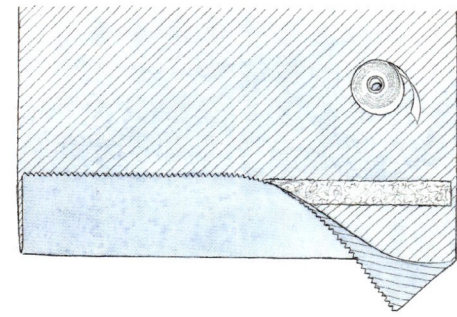

double-fold hem: Press one-half of the hem allowance to the wrong side of the fabric. Fold the remaining half to enclose the raw edge and press. To make a 2" (5.1 cm) double-fold hem, for example, you will fold 2" (5.1 cm) of the 4" (10.2 cm) hem allowance each time. Pin the folded edge in place. Stitch close to the inner folded edge through all layers.

machine blindstitch: Refer to your owner's manual for machine settings. Place the hem allowance facedown on the machine bed, with the rest of the fabric folded back. Leaving about $1/4$" (6 mm) of the hem edge extending beyond the fold. Align the fold against the guide in the foot. Stitch along the hem, close to the fold, catching only one or two threads of the fabric with each left-hand stitch. Open the fabric and press the hem flat.

fused hem: This hem style is suitable for lightweight woven fabrics. Test on scrap fabric first. Insert a strip of fusible web inside the hem. Steam-press, following the manufacturer's instructions.

If you are making a floor-length curtain, you may want to add drapery weights to stabilize the bottom of the curtain and improve the overall appearance. Hand-tack drapery weights into the corners of the panel, within the side seam allowance.

index